MORE SONGS OF THE FORTIES
THE DECADE SERIE

This publication is not for sale in
the EC and/or Australia
or New Zealand.

ISBN 0-7935-3093-8

HAL•LEONARD
CORPORATION

7777 W. BLUEMOUND RD. P.O. BOX 13819 MILWAUKEE, WI 53213

MORE SONGS OF THE FORTIES

THE DECADE SERIES

CONTENTS

AIR MAIL SPECIAL

Words and Music by BENNY GOODMAN,
CHARLIE CHRISTIAN and JIMMY MUNDY

Medium Swing Tempo

ALL THROUGH THE DAY

(From "CENTENNIAL SUMMER")

Lyrics by OSCAR HAMMERSTEIN II
Music by JEROME KERN

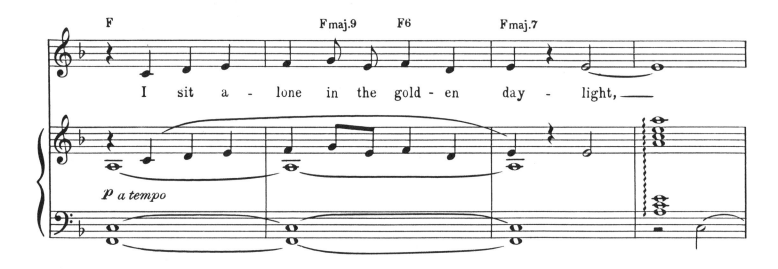

I sit a - lone in the gold - en day - light,

But all I see is a sil - ver sky; For in my

fan - cy I sweep a - way light,_____ And keep my

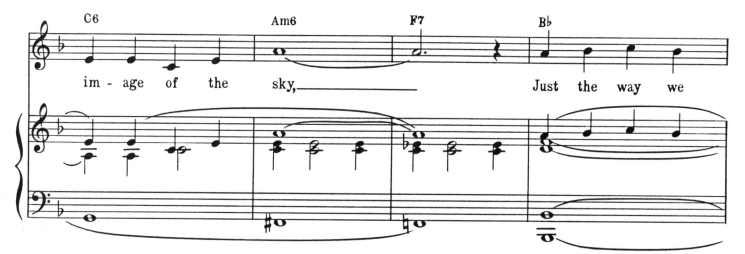

im - age of the sky,_____ Just the way we

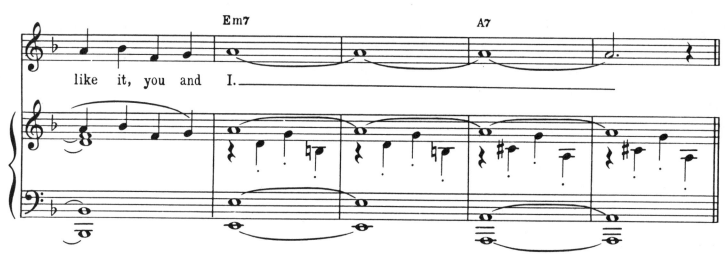

like it, you and I._____

Refrain - Moderato *(lyrically)*

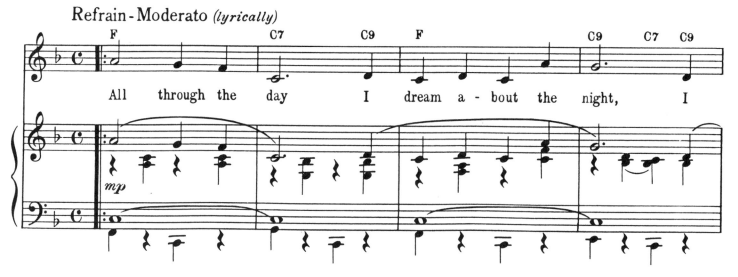

All through the day I dream a - bout the night, I

dream a - bout the night, Here with you.____

All through the day I wish a - way the time, Un -

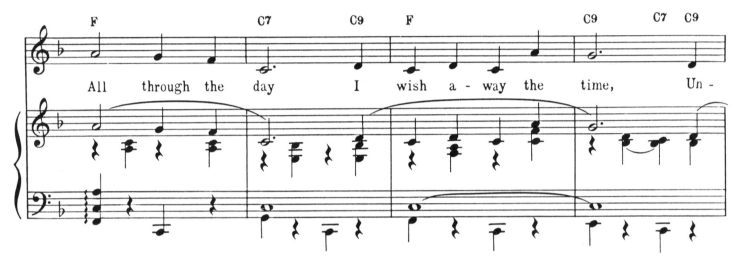

til the time when I'm here with you.____

with great breadth

Down falls the sun, I run to meet you,

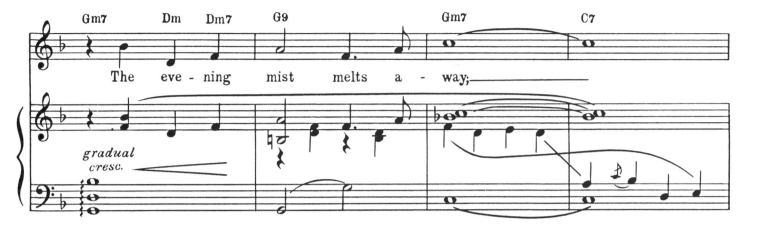

The eve-ning mist melts a - way;

Down smiles the moon, And soon your lips re - call The

kiss I dreamed of All through the day.

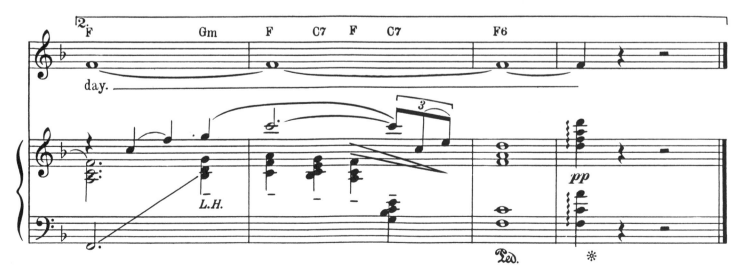

day.

ALWAYS TRUE TO YOU IN MY FASHION

(From "KISS ME KATE")

Words and Music by
COLE PORTER

Refrain *(graceful fox trot)*

If a cus-tom tail-ored vet ____ Asks me out for some-thing wet, ____
(From O) - hi - o, Mis - ter Thorne ____ Calls me up from night 'til morn, ____

When the vet be - gins to pet ____ I cry "Hoo - ray!"
Mis - ter Thorne once cor - nered corn ____ and that ain't hay, ____

But I'm al - ways true to you, ____
But I'm al - ways true to you, ____

— dar - lin', in my fash - ion, Yes, I'm
— dar - lin', in my fash - ion, Yes, I'm

al - ways true to you, —— dar - lin', in my way. ————
al - ways true to you, —— dar - lin', in my way. ————

I've been asked to have a meal —— By a
From Mil - wau - kee, Mis - ter Fritz —— Oft - en

big ty - coon in steel, —— If the meal in - cludes a deal, —
dines me at the Ritz, —— Mis - ter Fritz in - vent - ed Schlitz —

—— ac - cept I may, ———— But I'm
—— And Schlitz must pay! ———— But I'm

checks, I fear,— mean that "Tex" is here— to stay! _____
Har - ris pat— means a Pa - ris hat,— *Bé - bé! _____

But I'm al - ways true to you,— dar - lin', in my fash-ion,
But I'm al - ways true to you,— dar - lin', in my fash-ion,

Yes, I'm al - ways true to you, ___ dar - lin', in my way!
Yes, I'm al - ways true to you, ___ dar - lin', in my way!__

From O-

* Pronounced Baybay

AREN'T YOU KIND OF GLAD WE DID?

Music and Lyrics by
GEORGE and IRA GERSHWIN

aren't you kind of glad we did?—— Act - u - al - ly—— it all was
aren't you kind of glad we did?—— Peo - ple we know—— will call me

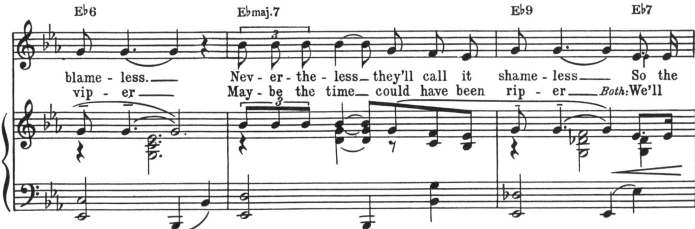

blame - less.—— Nev - er - the - less—— they'll call it shame - less—— So the
vip - er—— May - be the time—— could have been rip - er——Both: We'll

la - dy shall be name - less—— But aren't you kind a glad we did?
have to pay the pip - er—— But what we did we're glad we did——

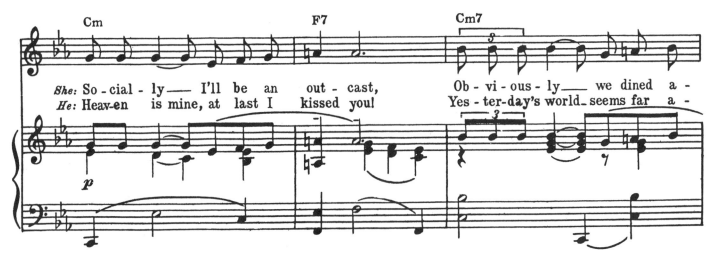

She: So - cial - ly—— I'll be an out - cast, Ob - vi - ous - ly—— we dined a -
He: Heav - en is mine, at last I kissed you! Yes - ter - day's world—— seems far a -

lone.
On my good name there will be doubt cast With
way. *She:* Truth-ful-ly I could not re - sist you, But

nev - er a sign of an - y chap-er - one *He:* No mat-ter how they may con -
what is it Mis - sis Grund-y's going to say? *He:* That I'm a cad, a Bos - ton

strue it, Wheth - er or not We have to rue it What - ev - er made us
bligh - ter Run - ning a - round with my type-writ-er. *Both:* Let's turn to some-thing

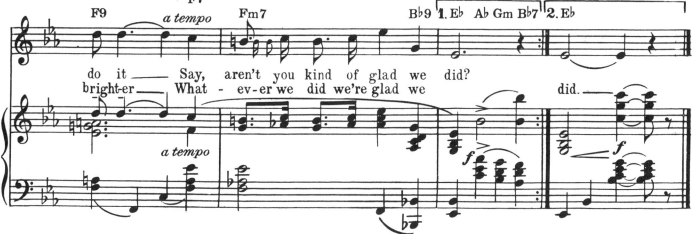

do it Say, aren't you kind of glad we did?
bright-er What - ev - er we did we're glad we did.

THE ANNIVERSARY WALTZ

Words and Music by AL DUBIN
and DAVE FRANKLIN

Moderately

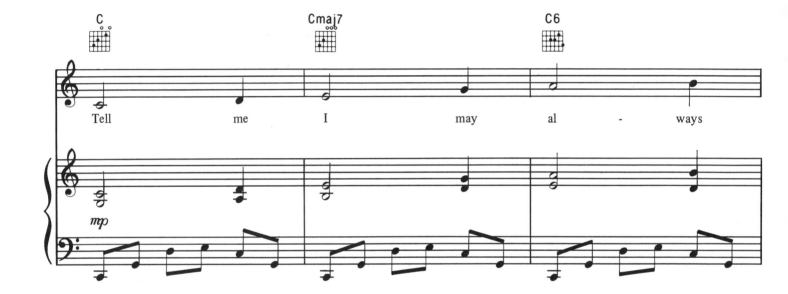

Tell me I may al - ways

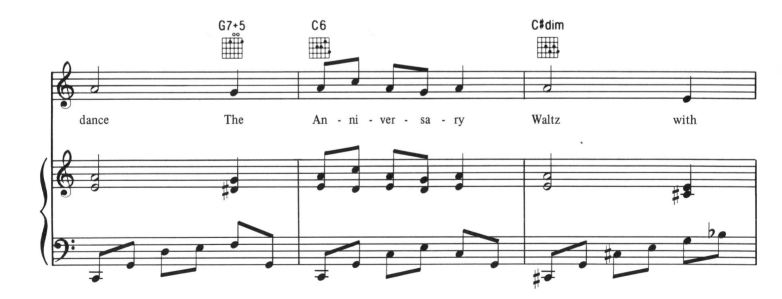

dance The An - ni - ver - sa - ry Waltz with

BALI HA'I
(From "SOUTH PACIFIC")

Lyrics by OSCAR HAMMERSTEIN II
Music by RICHARD RODGERS

BE CAREFUL, IT'S MY HEART

(From "HOLIDAY INN")

Words and Music by
IRVING BERLIN

burned. It's not the book I lent you that

you nev - er re - turned. Re -

mem - ber, _____ it's my heart. _____

The heart with which so will - ing - ly ____ I

BELL BOTTOM TROUSERS

Words and Music by
MOE JAFFE

Moderately Bright

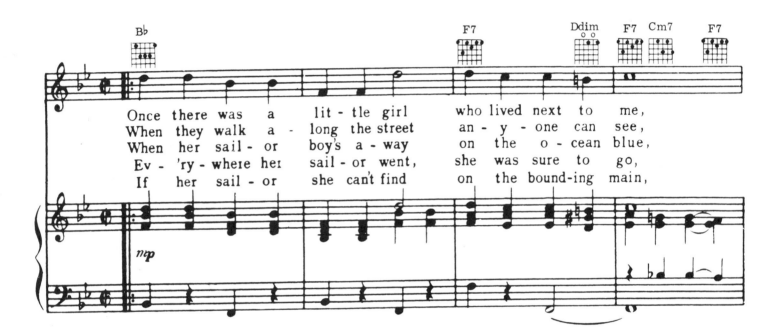

Once there was a lit-tle girl who lived next to me,
When they walk a - long the street an - y - one can see,
When her sail - or boy's a - way on the o - cean blue,
Ev - 'ry - where her sail - or went, she was sure to go,
If her sail - or she can't find on the bound-ing main,

And she loved a sail - or boy; he was on - ly three.
They are oh so much in love, hap - py as can be.
Sol - dier boys all flirt with her, but to him she's true,
Till one day he sailed a - way, where she does - n't know.
She is hope - ful he will soon come home safe a - gain.

Now he's on a bat-tle-ship in his sail-or suit,
Hand in hand they stroll a-long, they don't give a hoot,
Tho they smile and tip their caps, and they wink their eyes,
Now she's gon-na join the Waves may-be go to sea,
So they can get mar-ried, and raise a fa-mi-ly

Just a great big sail-or man but he's just as cute:
He won't let go of her hand, e-ven to sa-lute:
She just smiles and shakes her head; then she soft-ly sighs;
Try to find her sail-or boy wher-ev-er he may be:
Dress up all their kid-dies in sail-or's dun-ga-rees:

Chorus

BELL BOT-TOM TROU-SERS, coat of na-vy blue,

She loves her sail-or, and he loves her too too.

BIBBIDI-BOBBIDI-BOO
(THE MAGIC SONG)
(From Walt Disney's "CINDERELLA")

Words by JERRY LIVINGSTON
Music by MACK DAVID and AL HOFFMAN

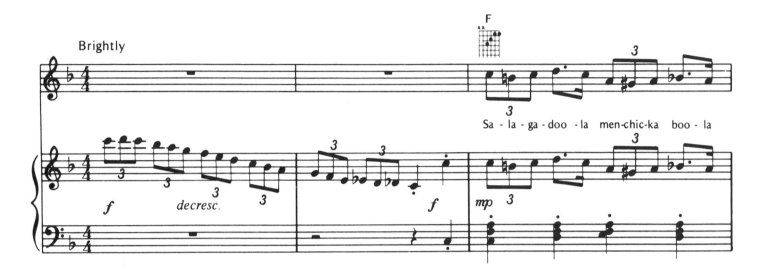

bib - bi - di - bob - bi - di - boo. Sa - la - ga - doo - la means men - chic - ka boo - le - roo, But the

thing - a - ma - bob that does the job is bib - bi - di - bob - bi - di - boo. Sa - la - ga - doo - la men - chic - ka boo la

bib - bi - di - bob - bi - di - boo Put 'em to - geth - er and what have you got

bib - bi - di - bob - bi - di bib - bi - di - bob - bi - di bib - bi - di - bob - bi - di - boo.

BLUE BIRD OF HAPPINESS

Words and Music by EDWARD HEYMAN
and SANDOR HARMATI

The beg-gar man and the might-y king are on-ly diff-'rent in name, For

they are treat-ed just the same by fate._____ To-

*) *Symbols for Guitar and Banjo*

hap - pi - ness.＿＿＿＿ You will find
hap - pi - ness.＿＿＿＿ When it's night,

Great - er peace of mind Know - ing there's a
Ev - 'ry - thing seems bright Since we found the

blue bird of hap - pi - ness.＿＿＿＿ And when he
blue, bird of hap - pi - ness.＿＿＿＿ Two hearts that

sings to you Though you're deep in blue,
beat as one 'Neath a new found sun,

BLUES IN THE NIGHT
(MY MAMA DONE TOL' ME)
(From "BLUES IN THE NIGHT")

Words by JOHNNY MERCER
Music by HAROLD ARLEN

BUTTONS AND BOWS
(From The Paramount Picture "PALEFACE")

Words and Music by JAY LIVINGSTON
and RAY EVANS

BOUQUET OF ROSES

Words and Music by STEVE NELSON
and BOB HILLIARD

Slowly

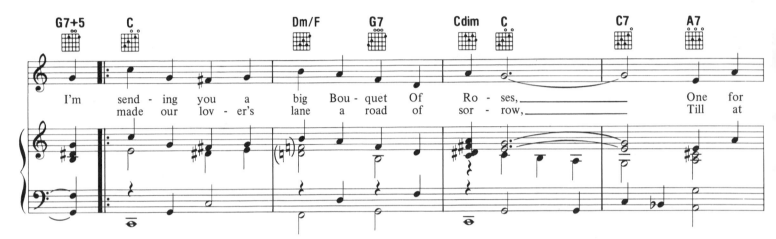

I'm send - ing you a big Bou - quet Of Ro - ses,_____ One for
made our lov - er's big lane a road Of sor - row,_____ Till at

ev - 'ry time you broke my heart,_____ And
last we had to say good - bye._____ You're

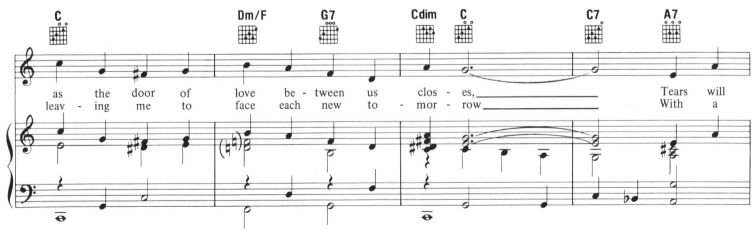

as the door of love be - tween us clos - es,_____ Tears will
leav - ing me to face each new to - mor - row_____ With a

CLOSE AS PAGES IN A BOOK

(From "UP IN CENTRAL PARK")

Words by DOROTHY FIELDS
Music by SIGMUND ROMBERG

Expressively

We'll be Close As Pag-es In A Book, My love and I.

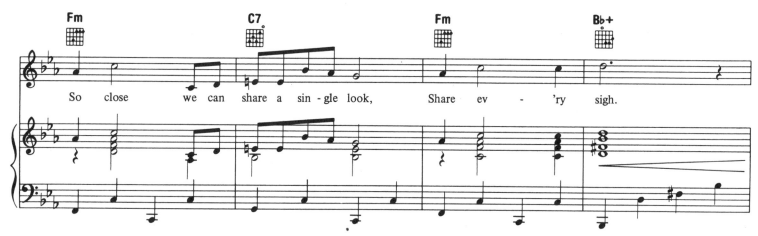

So close we can share a sin-gle look, Share ev-'ry sigh.

So close that be-fore I hear your laugh, My laugh breaks through;

CAN'T HELP SINGING
(From "CAN'T HELP SINGING")

Words by E.Y. HARBURG
Music by JEROME KERN

Gracefully

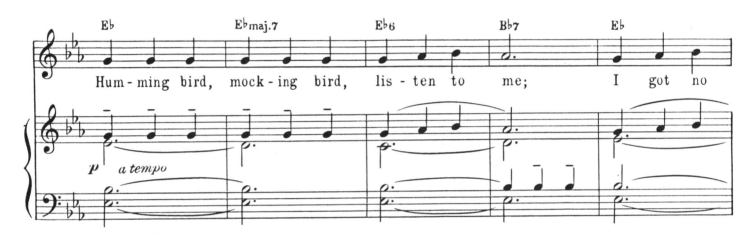

Hum-ming bird, mock-ing bird, lis-ten to me; I got no

nest, I got no tree. Oh, but I'm hap-py as

Heav-en is wide; I got a song bub-bling in - side:

Refrain *(in bright waltz tempo)*

Can't help sing - ing _____ of a

prom - ise that A - pril is bring - ing,_____ I am

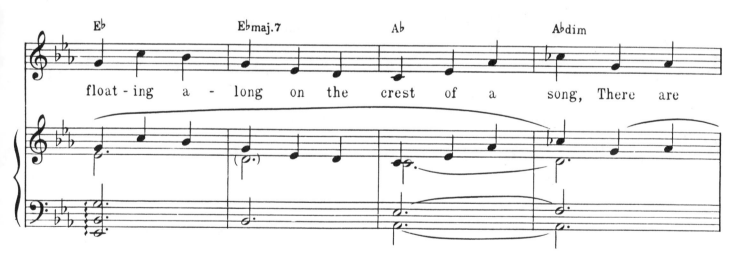

float - ing a - long on the crest of a song, There are

bells in my heart and they're ring - ing._____

DEARLY BELOVED

Music by JEROME KERN
Words by JOHNNY MERCER

58

Refrain-Andante cantabile, ma ben ritmato

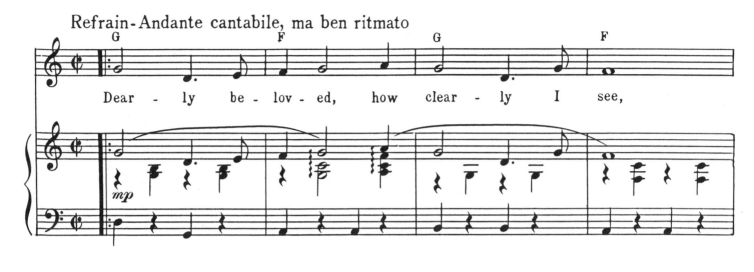

Dear - ly be - lov - ed, how clear - ly I see,

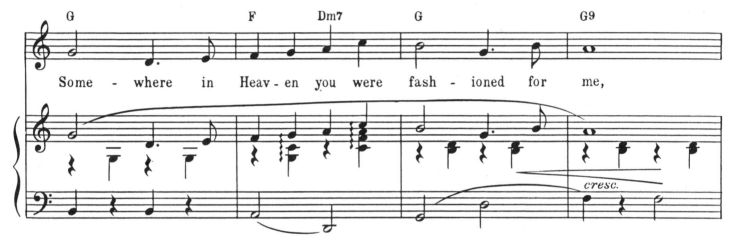

Some - where in Heav - en you were fash - ioned for me,

An - gel eyes _____ knew you, _____

An - gel voi - ces led me to you; _____

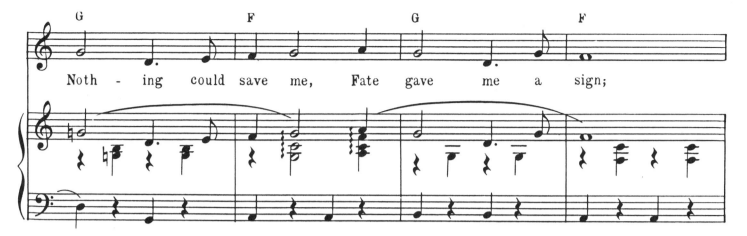

Noth - ing could save me, Fate gave me a sign;

I know that I'll be yours come show - er or shine;

So I say _____ mere - ly, _____ Dear - ly be -

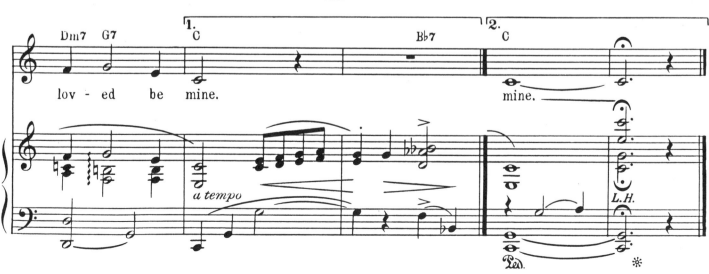

lov - ed be mine.   mine.

DAY BY DAY
(Theme From The Paramount Television Series "DAY BY DAY")

Words and Music by SAMMY CAHN,
AXEL STORDAHL and PAUL WESTON

Moderately slow, expressively

DAY BY DAY___ I'm fall-ing more in love with you, And DAY BY DAY___

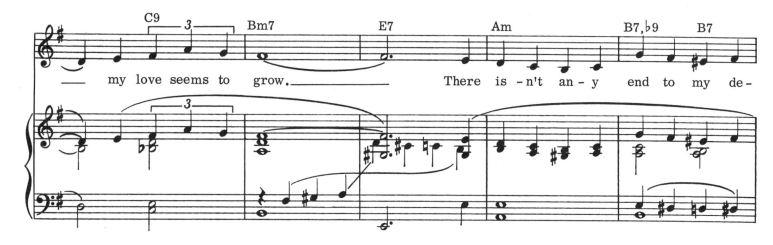

___ my love seems to grow.___ There is-n't an-y end to my de-

vo-tion,___ It's deep-er, dear, by far, than an-y o-cean.

I find that DAY BY DAY___ you're mak-ing all my dreams come true, So

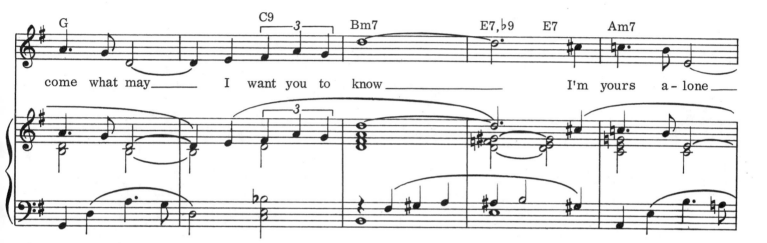

come what may___ I want you to know___ I'm yours a-lone___

___ and I'm in love to stay, As we go through the years, DAY BY

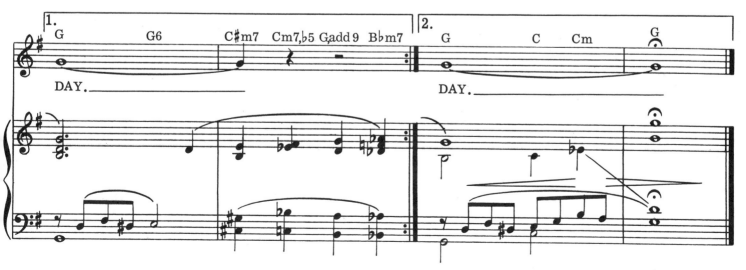

DAY._____ DAY._____

A DREAM IS A WISH YOUR HEART MAKES

(From Walt Disney's "CINDERELLA")

Words and Music by MACK DAVID,
AL HOFFMAN and JERRY LIVINGSTON

DON'T EXPLAIN

Words and Music by BILLIE HOLIDAY
and ARTHUR HERZOG

MCA music publishing

FIVE GUYS NAMED MOE

Words and Music by LARRY WYNN
and JERRY BRESLER

MCA music publishing

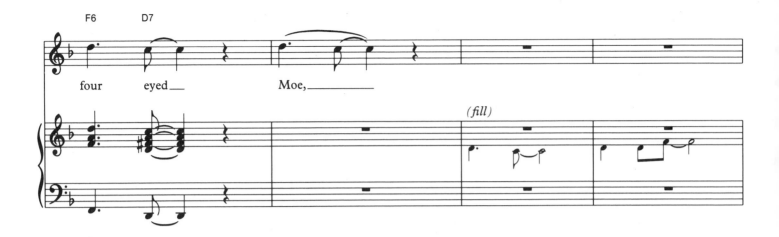

four eyed Moe,

no Moe,

(fill)

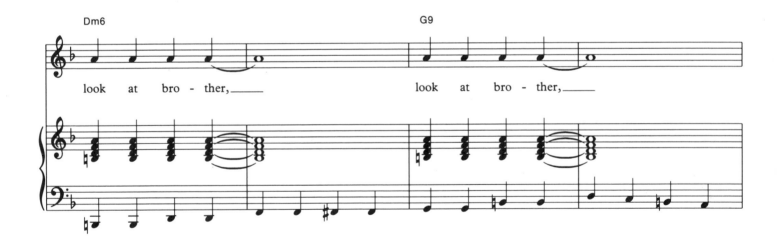

look at bro-ther, look at bro-ther,

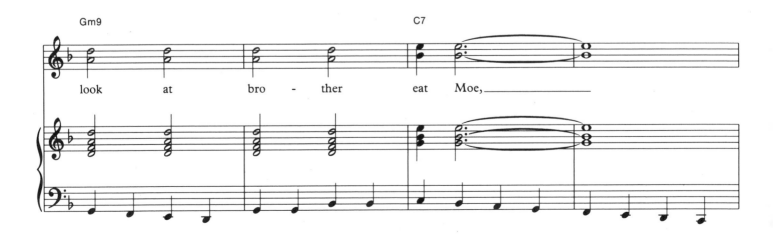

look at bro - ther eat Moe,

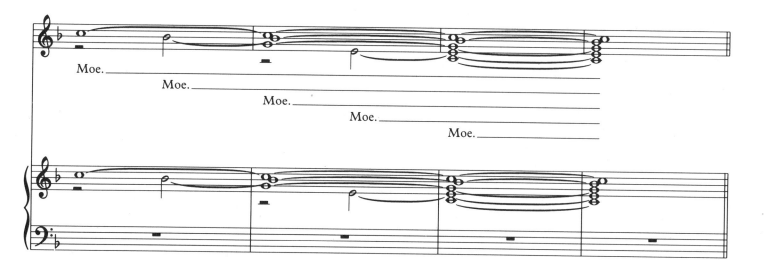

Moe. _____
Moe. _____
Moe. _____
Moe. _____
Moe. _____

Who's the great-est band a-round, makes the cats jump up and down, _

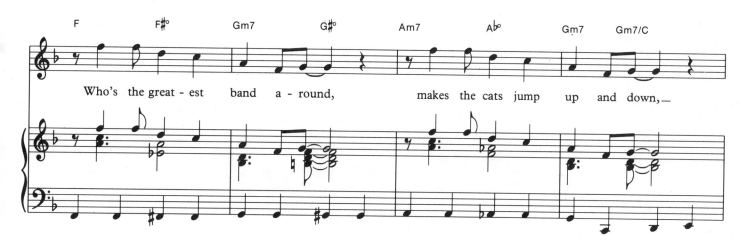

who's the talk of rhy-thm town, _ five guys named Moe, that's us.

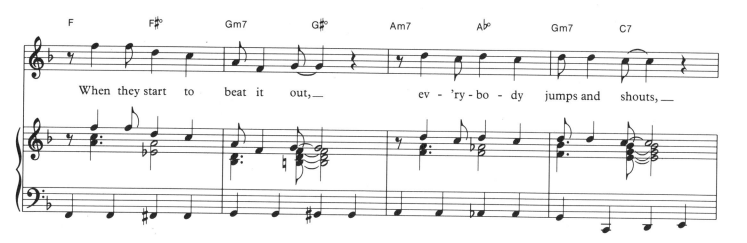

When they start to beat it out, _ ev-'ry-bo-dy jumps and shouts, _

tell me who the cri-tics all rave a-bout___ five guys named Moe, Ah!

We came out of no-where that don't mean a thing.

We rate high___ and you'll know why___ when you hear us sing,_____

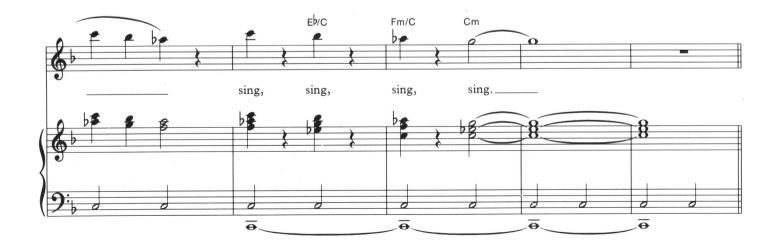

_____ sing, sing, sing, sing._____

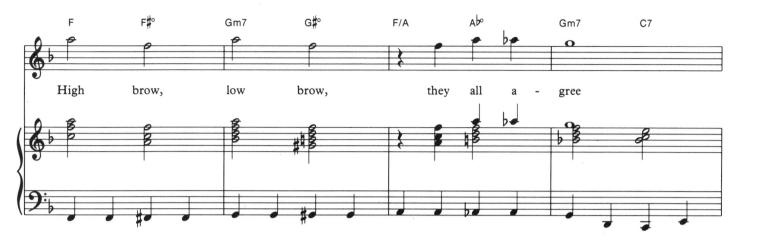

High brow, low brow, they all a - gree

we're the best in har - mo - ny_____ I'm

D.S al Coda

tell-ing you folks,_ you real - ly ought to see five guys named Moe.

CODA

sing._____

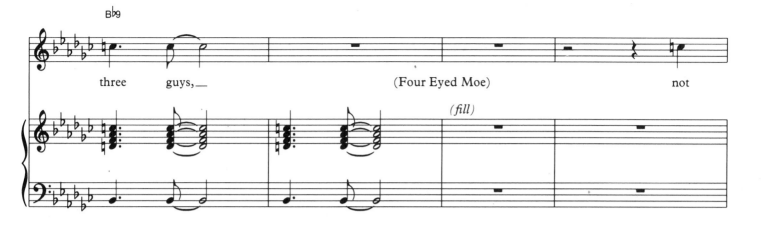

three guys, ___ (Four Eyed Moe) not

four guys, ___ (Big Moe) but five guys, ___

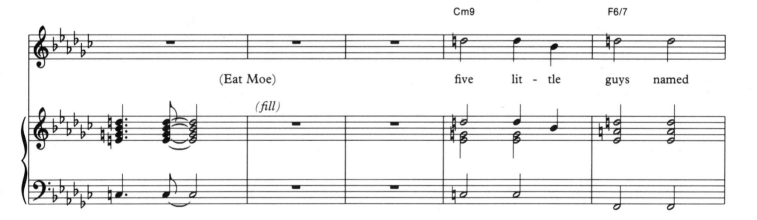

(Eat Moe) five lit - tle guys named

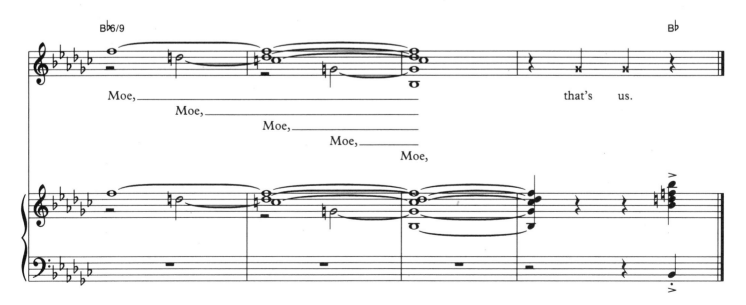

Moe, _____ that's us.
Moe, _____
Moe, _____
Moe, _____
Moe,

EV'RY TIME WE SAY GOODBYE

(From "SEVEN LIVELY ARTS")

Words and Music by
COLE PORTER

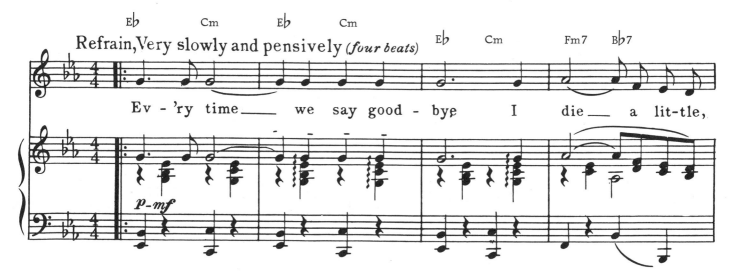

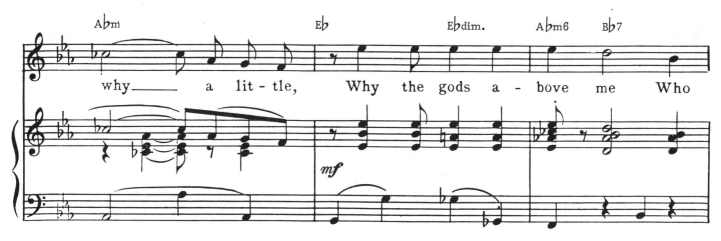

fin - er, But how strange the change from ma - jor to mi - nor

Ev - 'ry time____ we say good - bye.____

we say good - bye. Ev - 'ry sin - gle time____ we

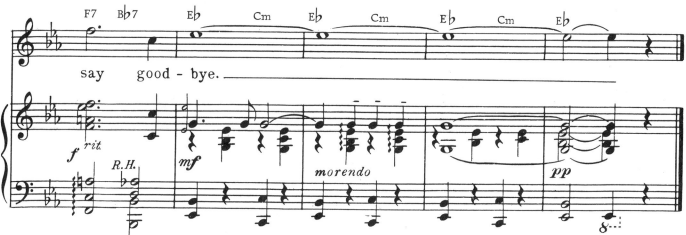

say good - bye._____

CHIQUITA BANANA

Words and Music by LEN MACKENZIE,
GARTH MONTGOMERY and WILLIAM WIRGES

THE GIRL THAT I MARRY

(From The Stage Production "ANNIE GET YOUR GUN")

Words and Music by
IRVING BERLIN

GIVE A LITTLE WHISTLE

(From "PINOCCHIO")

Words by NED WASHINGTON
Music by LEIGH HARLINE

When you get in trou - ble and you don't know right from wrong; } Give a lit - tle
When you meet tem - ta - tion, and the urge is ver - y strong;

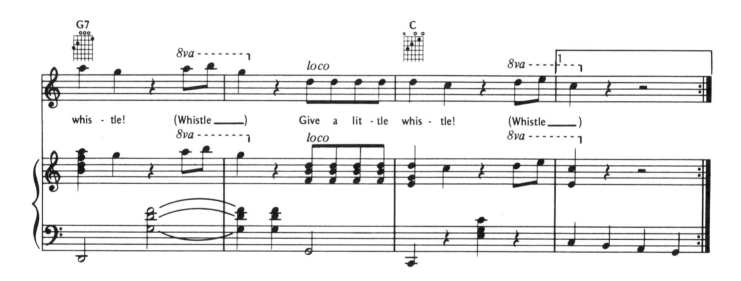

whis - tle!   (Whistle ____)   Give a lit - tle whis - tle!   (Whistle ____)

Not   just a lit - tle squeak;   Puck - er up and

PUT THE BLAME ON MAME

Words and Music by ALLAN ROBERTS
and DORIS FISHER

Piano score by Marvin Fisher

Extra Choruses

When they had the gold rush folks started running to Cal-i-for-ni-ay,
They all had dreams of making a million bucks a day.
That's the story that went around but here's the real low down:
"Put The Blame On Mame," boys, "Put The Blame On Mame."
She caused the gold rush, It's my belief,
Diggin' gold from some guy's teeth.
So you can "Put The Blame On Mame," boys, "Put The Blame On Mame."

Remember the blizzard back in Manhattan, in eighteen-eighty-six?
They say the traffic was tied up and folks were in a fix.
That's the story that went around but here's the real low down:
"Put The Blame On Mame," boys, "Put The Blame On Mame."
Mame gave a chump such an ice-cold no,
For seven days they shoveled snow.
So you can "Put The Blame On Mame," boys, "Put The Blame On Mame."

There was once a shootin' up in the Klondike when they got Dan Magrew
Folks were puttin' the blame on the lady known as "Lou."
That's the story that went around but here's the real low down:
"Put The Blame On Mame," boys, "Put The Blame On Mame."
Mame did a dance and she dropped her fan
That's the thing that murdered Dan
So you can "Put The Blame On Mame," boys, "Put The Blame On Mame."

HEARTACHES

Words by JOHN KLENNER
Music by AL HOFFMAN

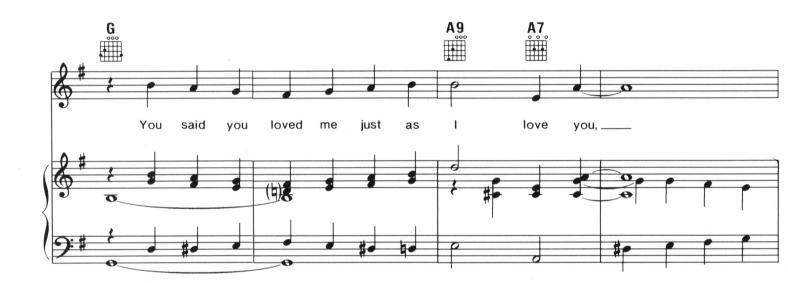

You said you loved me just as I love you, ___

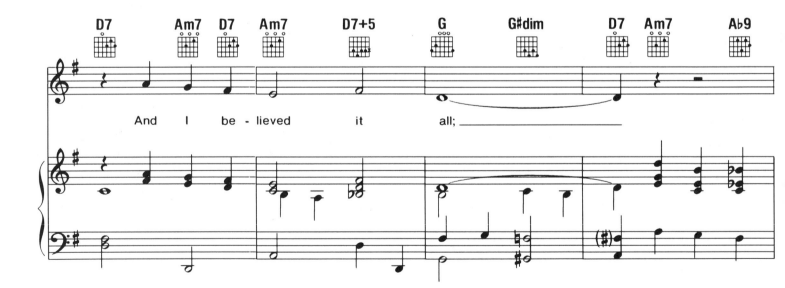

And I be-lieved it all; ___

MCA music publishing

HIT THE ROAD TO DREAMLAND

(From The Paramount Picture "STAR SPANGLED RHYTHM")

Words by JOHNNY MERCER
Music by HAROLD ARLEN

*Chord Names For Guitar

I CAIN'T SAY NO!

(From "OKLAHOMA!")

Lyrics by OSCAR HAMMERSTEIN II
Music by RICHARD RODGERS

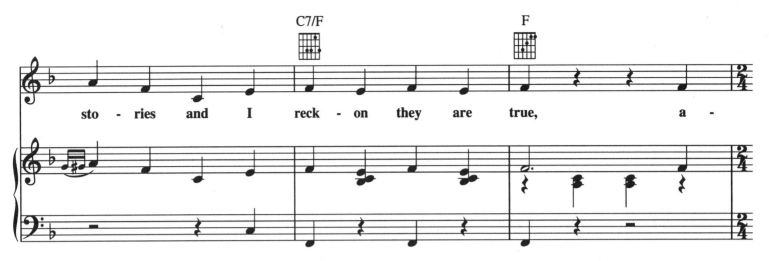

sto - ries and I reck - on they are true, a -

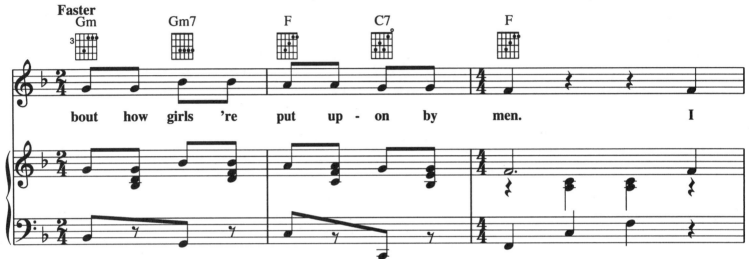

Faster

bout how girls 're put up - on by men. I

know I must - n't fall in - to the pit. _____ but

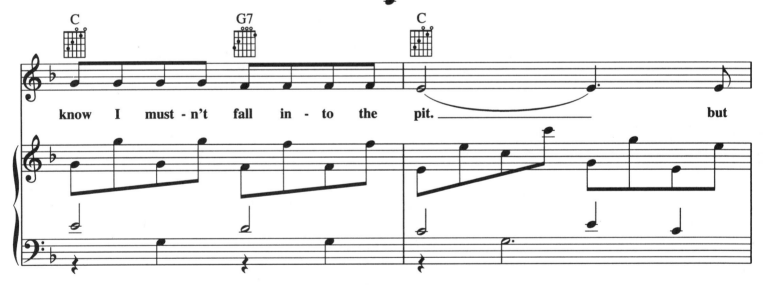

Lively

when I'm with a fel - ler, I fer - git!

I HAD MYSELF A TRUE LOVE

(From "ST. LOUIS WOMAN")

Words by JOHNNY MERCER
Music by HAROLD ARLEN

Slowly and with tenderness

I had my-self a true love, a true love who was some-thin' to see.

I had my-self a true love, at

least that's what I kept on tell-in' me, The

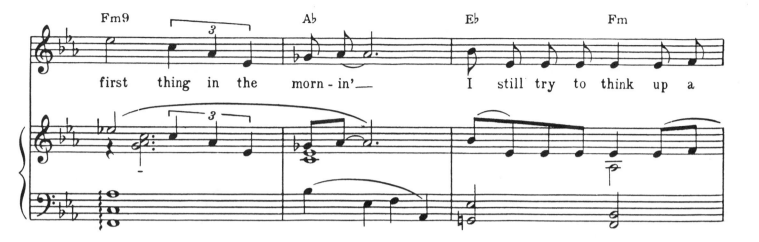

hum - min',_____ Where is he, while I watch the ris - in' moon?_____ With that gal in that damn ol' sa - loon?_____

No! _____ That ain' the way that it used to be.

No! _____

An' ev-'ry-bod-y keeps tell-in' me,_____ There may_ be a lot o'

things I miss, A lot o' things I don't know, but I do know this:

Now I ain' got no love an' once up-on a time I had a true_ love.____

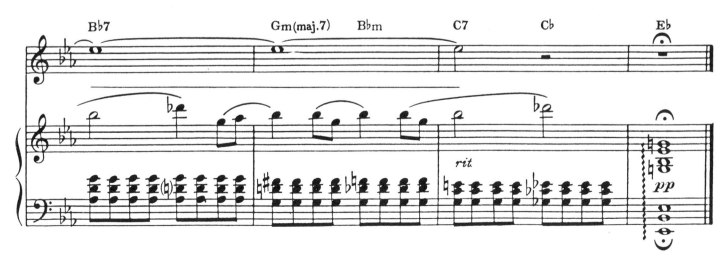

I HATE YOU, DARLING

(From "LET'S FACE IT")

Words and Music by
COLE PORTER

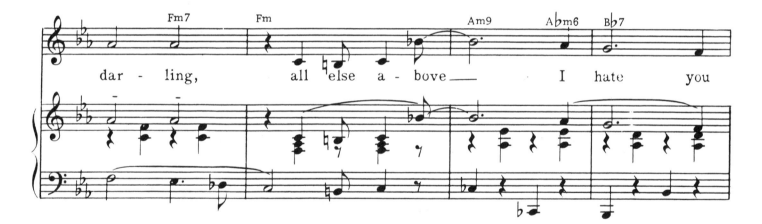

I should be clev - er

and say "good-bye," Good-bye, for - ev - er, my but-ter-fly.

But why be clev - er, When dar-ling I___ need The

joy you bring more than an - y - thing I know.___ I'm in the

It's true my pet— I hate you dar - ling

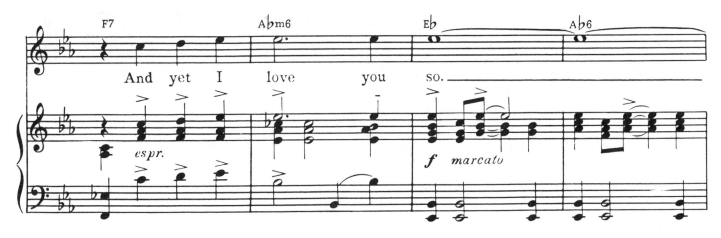

But don't for - get— I hate you dar - ling

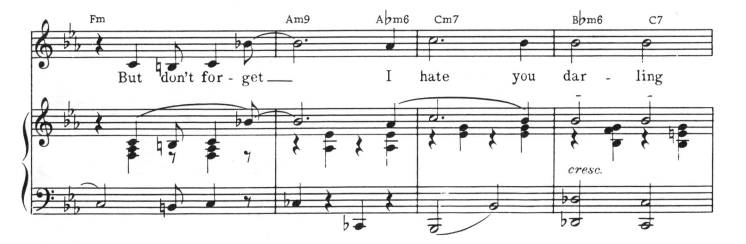

And yet I love you so.—

I

I LOVE YOU

Words and Music by
COLE PORTER

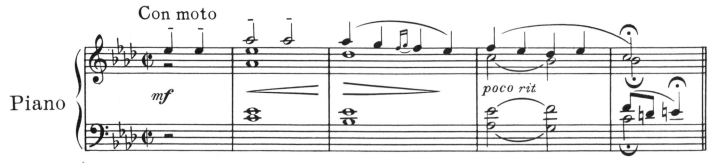

If a love song I could on-ly write,____ A song with words and

mu-sic di - vine____ I would ser - e - nade you ev - 'ry

night ____ Till you'd re - lent and con - sent to be mine ____ But a-

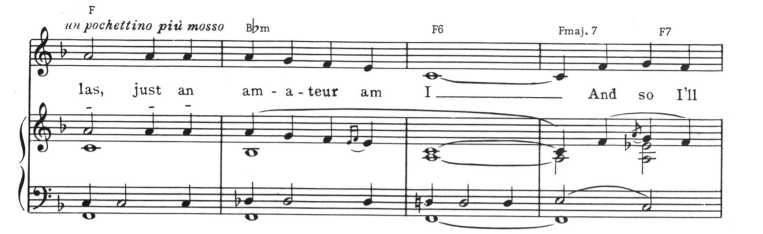

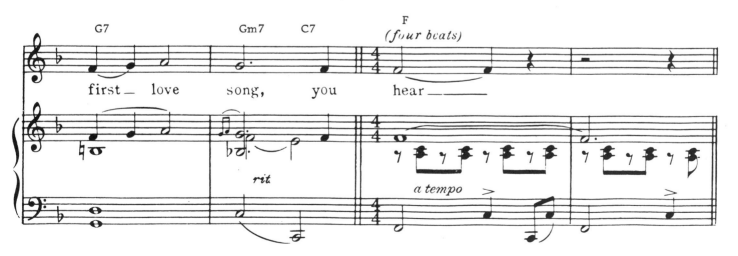

114

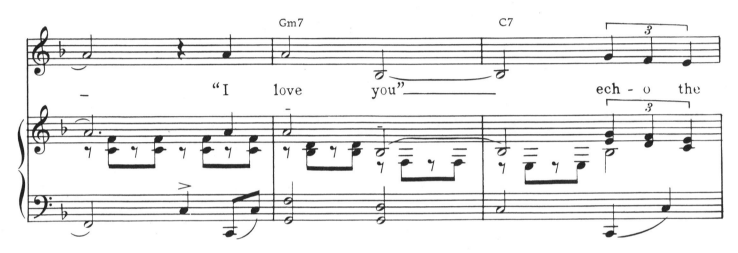

more she sees daf - fo - dils.

— It's spring a - gain _____ And birds on the

wing a - gain _____ start to sing a - gain _____

— The old mel - o - die _____ "I

love you" That's the song of songs, And it

all be-longs to you and me. I

me And it all be-longs to you and

me.

DIAMONDS ARE A GIRL'S BEST FRIEND

from GENTLEMEN PREFER BLONDES

Words by LEO ROBIN
Music by JULE STYNE

I'M JUST A LUCKY SO AND SO

Words and Music by MACK DAVID
and DUKE ELLINGTON

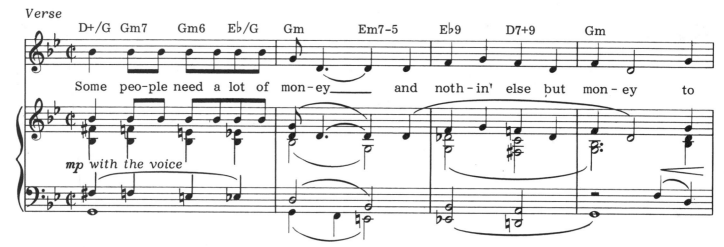

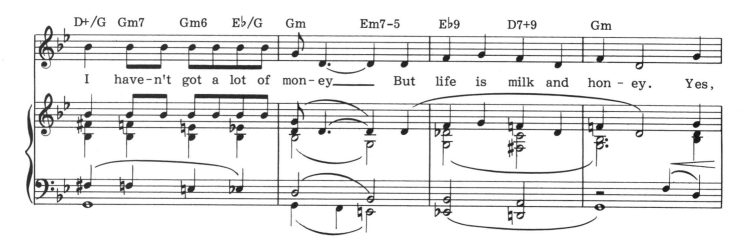

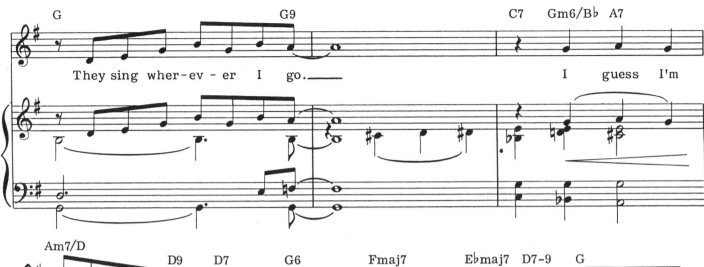

They sing wher-ev-er I go.___ I guess I'm

just a luck-y so-and-so.___ If you should

ask me the a-mount In my bank ac-count, I'd have to con-fess___ that I'm

slip-pin'.___ But that don't wor-ry me, con-fi-den-tial-ly, I've got a

I'M OLD FASHIONED

(From "YOU WERE NEVER LOVELIER")

Words by JOHNNY MERCER
Music by JEROME KERN

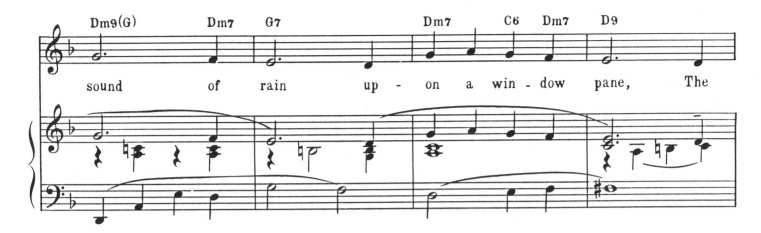

sound of rain up - on a win - dow pane, The

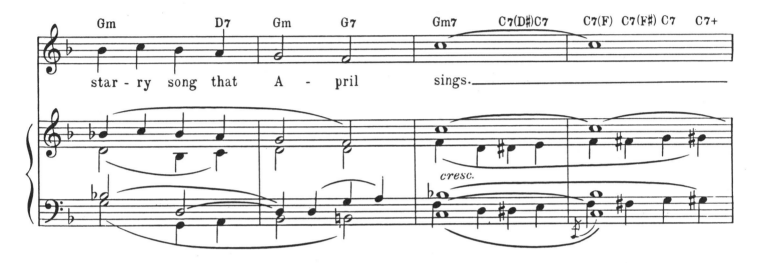

star - ry song that A - pril sings.____

This year's fan - cies are pass - ing fan - cies, But

sigh - ing sighs, hold - ing hands,___ These my heart un - der - stands.

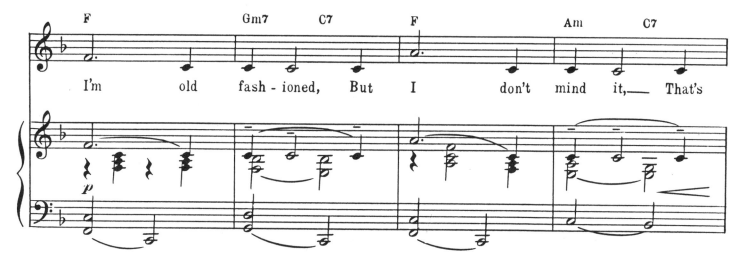

I'm old fash-ioned, But I don't mind it,___ That's

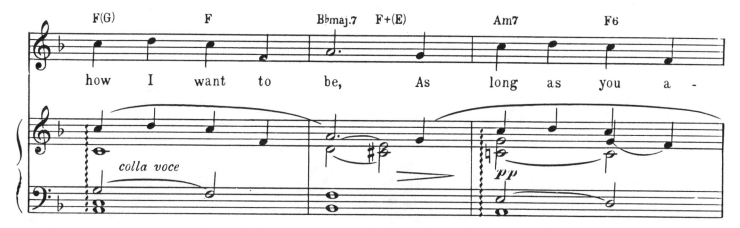

how I want to be, As long as you a-

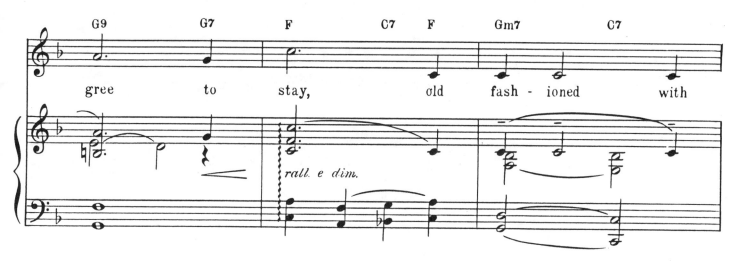

gree to stay, old fash-ioned with

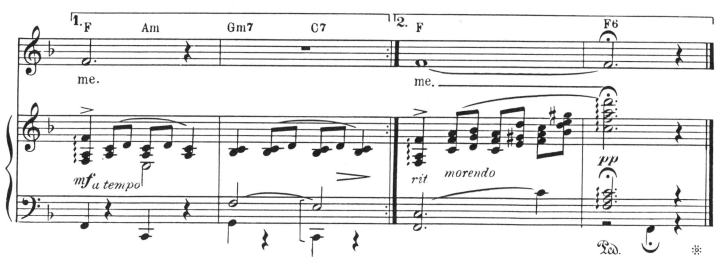

1. me. 2. me.___

IS YOU IS, OR IS YOU AIN'T
(MA' BABY)

Words and Music by BILLY AUSTIN
and LOUIS JORDAN

Is you is or is you ain't my ba-by?__ The

way you're act-ing late-ly makes me doubt.__

Is__ you is or is you ain't my ba-by?__

Seems my flame in your heart's done gone out.__ My

MCA music publishing

friends say I could do a lot bet - ter,__ if this keeps up I'll soon need a nurse.__ I

know I can't do a-ny bet-ter,__ but be-lieve me I could do a lot worse.__

Is__ you is or is you ain't my ba - by?__ The

way you're act-ing late-ly makes me doubt.__

Is__ you is or is you ain't my ba - by?_____

Seems my flame in your heart's done gone out._____ When the

moon goes down in the dawn - ing__ and the sun comes up in the morn -

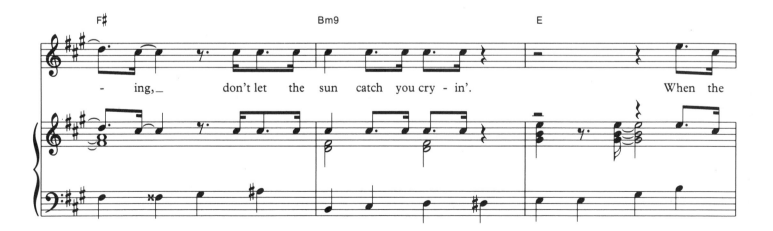

- ing,__ don't let the sun catch you cry - in'. When the

moon goes down in the dawn - ing,_ don't let the sun catch you cry - in' if your

ba - by don't want_ you no more._ No_ more.

No_ more._

IT MIGHT AS WELL BE SPRING
(From "STATE FAIR")

Lyrics by OSCAR HAMMERSTEIN II
Music by RICHARD RODGERS

JAVA JIVE

Lightly, with an easy beat

Words and Music by MILTON DRAKE
and BEN OAKLAND

I love cof-fee, I love tea,___ I love the ja-va jive and it loves me.___

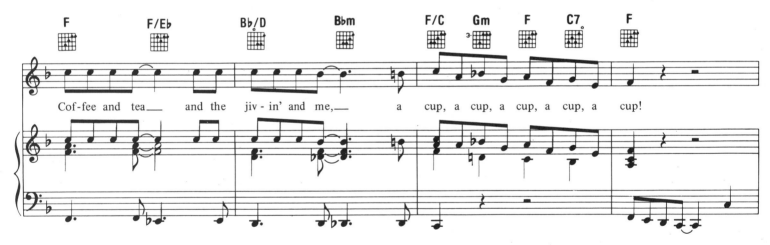

Cof-fee and tea___ and the jiv-in' and me,___ a cup, a cup, a cup, a cup, a cup!

I love ja-va, sweet and hot,___ Whoops! Mis-ter Mo-to, I'm a cof-fee pot.___

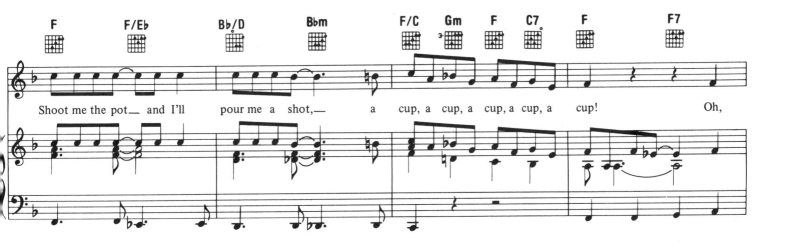

Shoot me the pot __ and I'll pour me a shot, __ a cup, a cup, a cup, a cup, a cup! Oh,

slip me a slug __ from that won - der-ful mug, __ and I'll cut a rug, __ till I'm snug __ in the jug. __

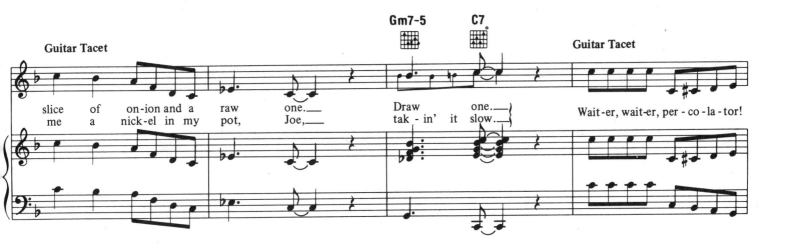

Guitar Tacet

slice of on-ion and a raw one. __ Draw one. __ Wait-er, wait-er, per - co-la-tor!
me a nick-el in my pot, Joe, __ tak - in' it slow.

Guitar Tacet

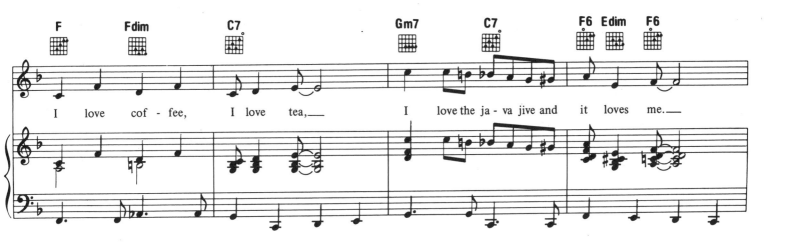

I love cof - fee, I love tea, __ I love the ja - va jive and it loves me. __

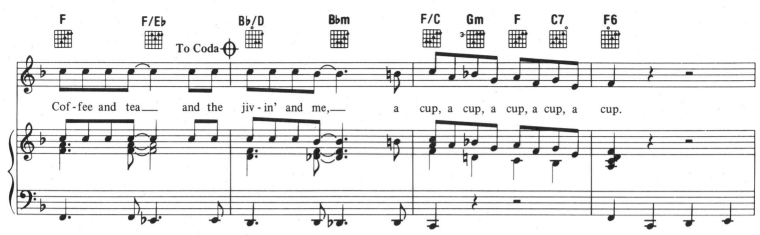

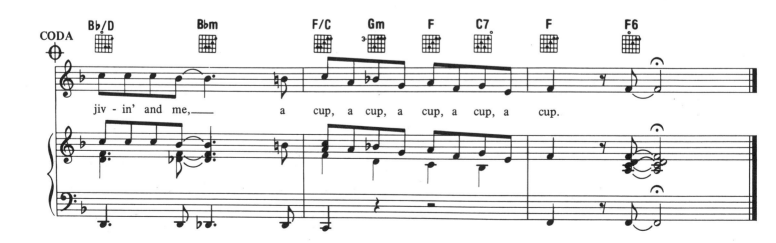

LONG AGO
(AND FAR AWAY)
(From "COVER GIRL")

Words by IRA GERSHWIN
Music by JEROME KERN

Moderately

Con moto

Drear-y days are o-ver. Life's a four-leaf clo-ver.

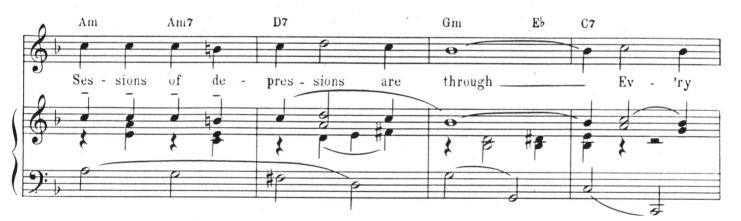

Ses-sions of de-pres-sions are through _____ Ev-'ry

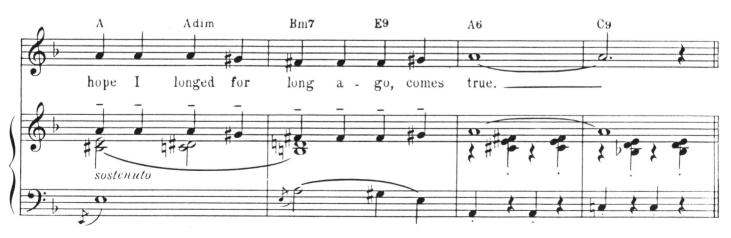

hope I longed for long a-go, comes true. _____

Refrain *(cantabile)*

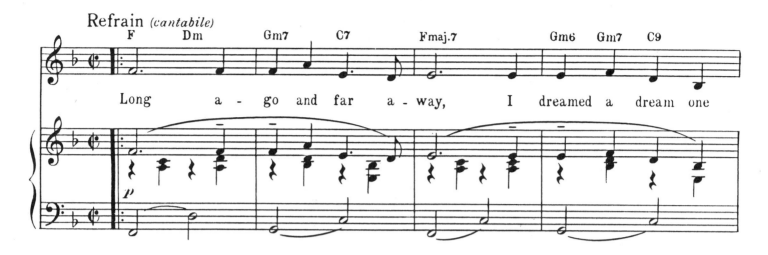

Long a - go and far a - way, I dreamed a dream one

day And now that dream is here be - side me.

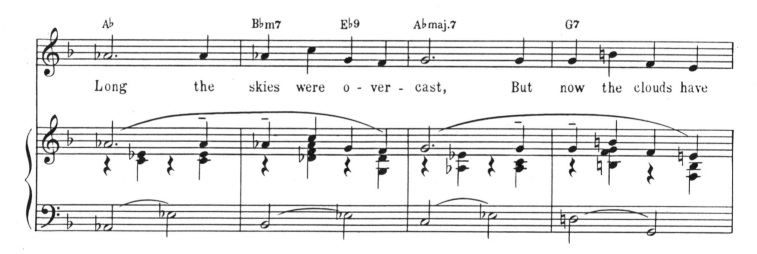

Long the skies were o - ver - cast, But now the clouds have

passed: You're here at last! _____ Chills run

up and down my spine, A - lad - din's lamp is mine, The dream I

dreamed was not de - nied me. Just one look and then I

knew ———— That all I longed for long a - go, was

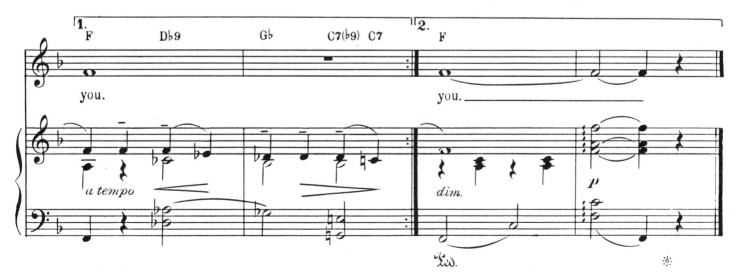

1. you. 2. you. ————

KANSAS CITY
(From "OKLAHOMA!)

Lyrics by OSCAR HAMMERSTEIN II
Music by RICHARD RODGERS

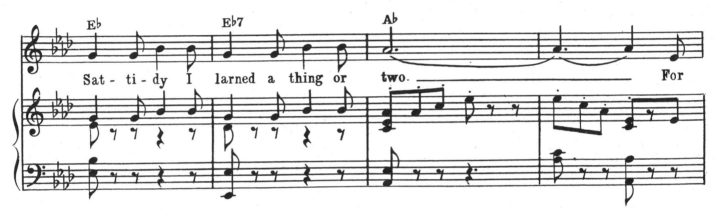

count - ed twen - ty gas bug - gies go - in' by their - sels'

Al - most ev - 'ry time I tuk a walk.———

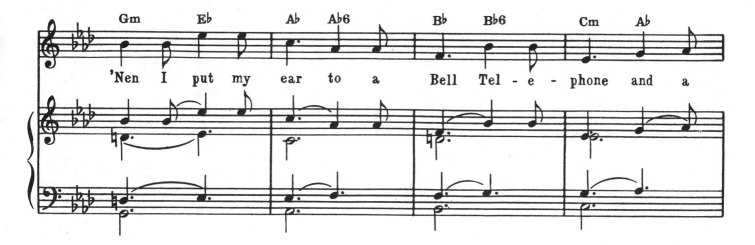

'Nen I put my ear to a Bell Tel - e - phone and a

strange wom - ern start - ed in to talk!——————— (Whut

next! Yeah whut!) Whut next?

Refrain

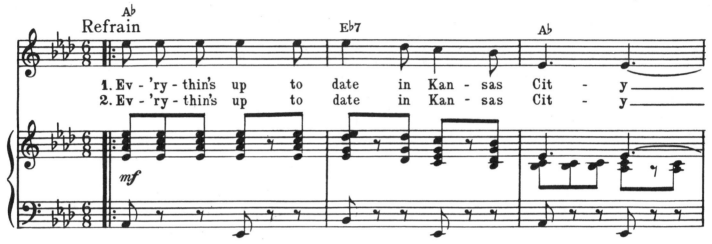

1. Ev - 'ry - thin's up to date in Kan - sas Cit - y
2. Ev - 'ry - thin's up to date in Kan - sas Cit - y

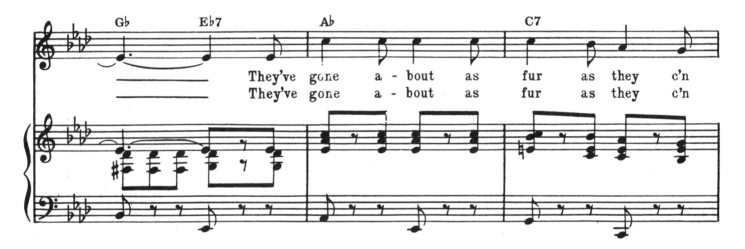

_____ They've gone a - bout as fur as they c'n
_____ They've gone a - bout as fur as they c'n

go! _____
go! _____
They went and built a
They got a big the -

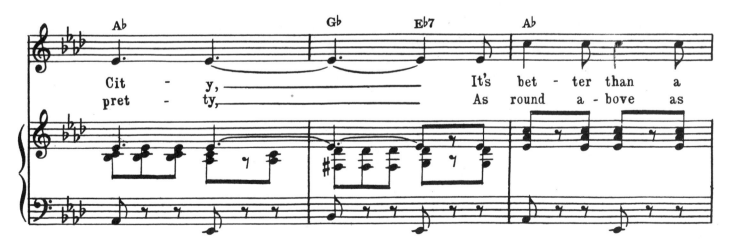

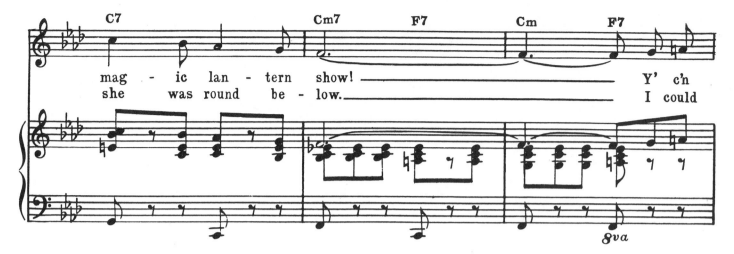

mag - ic lan - tern show! _____ Y' c'n
she was round be - low. _____ I could

turn the rad - i - a - tor on when ev - er you want some
swear that she was pad - ded from her shoul - der to her

heat. ____ With ev - 'ry kind o' com - fort ev - 'ry
heel, ____ But lat - er in the sec - ond act when

house is all com - plete. ____ You c'n walk to priv - ies
she be - gan to peel ____ She proved that ev - 'ry -

in the rain and nev - er wet your feet! They've
thin' she had was ab - so - lute - ly real! She

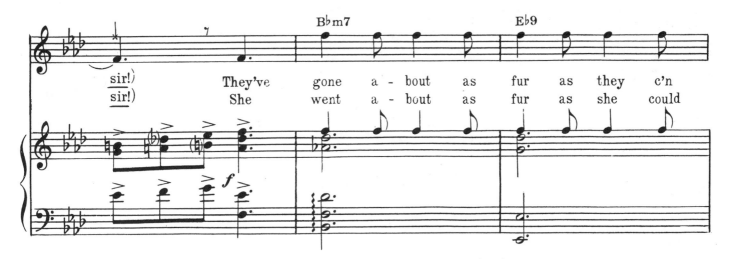

gone a - bout as fur as they c'n go, _____ (Yes
went a - bout as fur as she could go, _____ (Yes

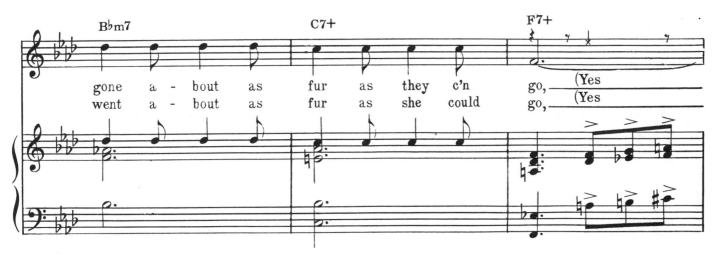

sir!)
sir!)

They've gone a - bout as fur as they c'n
She went a - bout as fur as she could

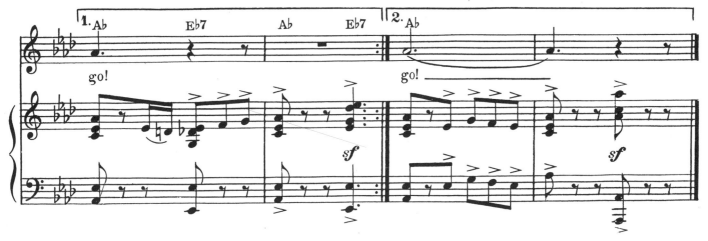

go!

go!

BYE-BYE BABY

from GENTLEMEN PREFER BLONDES

Words by LEO ROBIN
Music by JULE STYNE

Moderately with expression

LOOK TO THE RAINBOW

(From "FINIAN'S RAINBOW")

Words by E.Y. HARBURG
Music by BURTON LANE

Moderately

Eb **Cm** **Fm7**

mp

Bb7 **Eb**

On the day I was born, said my fa - ther, said
sump - tu - ous gift to be - queath to a
bun - dled me heart and I roamed the world

he, I've an el - e - gant leg - a - cy
child, oh the lure of that song kept her
free, to the east with the lark, to the

Ab **Bb** **Bb7/D**

wait - in' for ye. 'Tis a rhyme for your
feet run - nin' wild. For you nev - er grow
west with the sea. And I searched all the

MAD ABOUT HIM, SAD WITHOUT HIM, HOW CAN I BE GLAD WITHOUT HIM BLUES

Words and Music by LARRY MARKES
and DICK CHARLES

I went to bed last eve-nin' feel-in' blue as I could be ___

MOONLIGHT BECOMES YOU

(From The Paramount Picture "ROAD TO MOROCCO")

Words by JOHNNY BURKE
Music by JAMES VAN HEUSEN

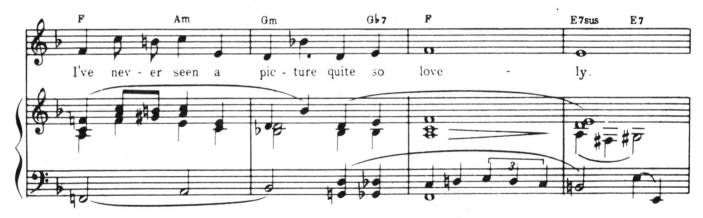

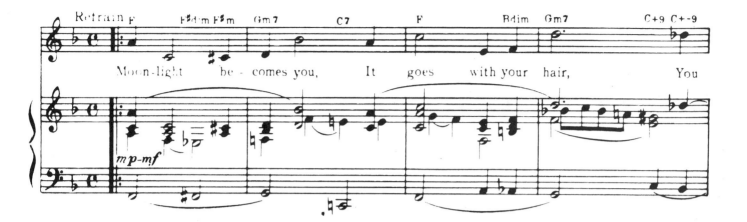

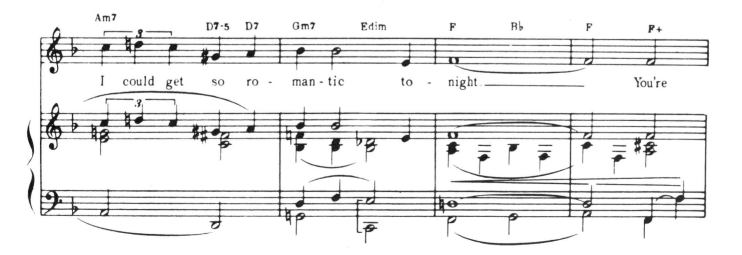

all dressed up to go dream-ing, Now don't tell me I'm wrong, And what a night to go

dream-ing, Mind if I tag a - long? If I say I love you, I

want you to know It's not just be-cause there's moon-light, al-though

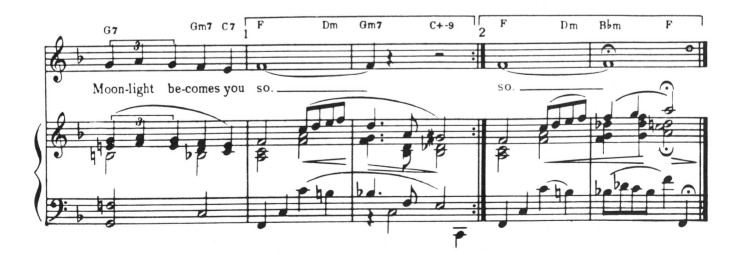

Moon-light be-comes you so. _____ so. _____

THE NEARNESS OF YOU

(From The Paramount Picture "ROMANCE IN THE DARK")

Words by NED WASHINGTON
Music by HOAGY CARMICHAEL

THIS IS MY COUNTRY

Words by DON RAYE
Music by AL JACOBS

THE OLD PIANO ROLL BLUES

Words and Music by
CY COBEN

* Symbols for Guitar. Diagrams for Ukulele

MCA music publishing

PISTOL PACKIN' MAMA

Words and Music by
AL DEXTER

Moderate Blues Tempo

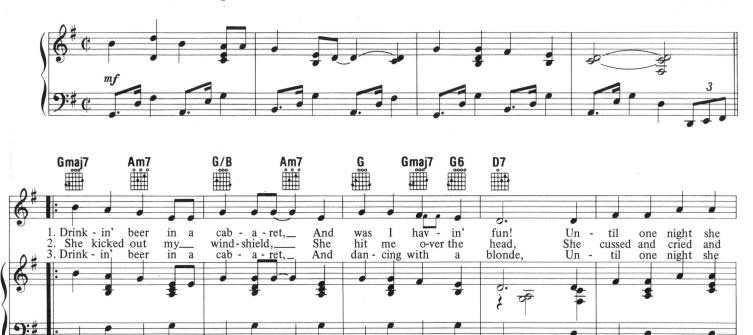

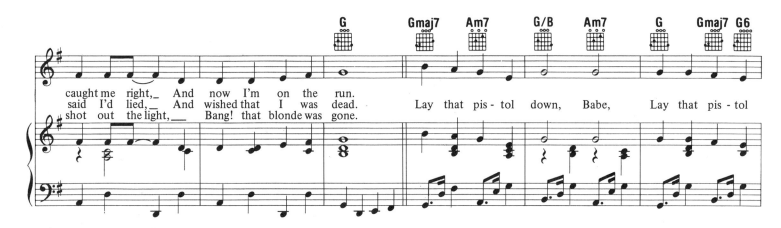

1. Drink-in' beer in a cab-a-ret,__ And was I hav-in' fun! Un-til one night she
2. She kicked out my__ wind-shield,__ She hit me o-ver the head, She cussed and cried and
3. Drink-in' beer in a cab-a-ret,__ And danc-ing with a blonde, Un-til one night she

caught me right,__ And now I'm on the run.
said I'd lied,__ And wished that I was dead.
shot out the light,__ Bang! that blonde was gone.

Lay that pis-tol down, Babe, Lay that pis-tol

down, Pis-tol Pack-in' Ma-ma, Lay that pis-tol down! down!

PRAISE THE LORD AND PASS THE AMMUNITION!

Words and Music by
FRANK LOESSER

CHORUS

"Praise the Lord and pass the am-mu-ni-tion! Praise the Lord and pass the am-mu ni-tion!

Praise the Lord and pass the am-mu-ni-tion, and we'll all stay free! Praise the Lord and

swing in-to po-si-tion. Can't af-ford to sit a-round a'-wish-in'. Praise the Lord; we're

all be-tween per-di-tion and the deep blue sea!" Yes, the sky pi-lot said it. You've

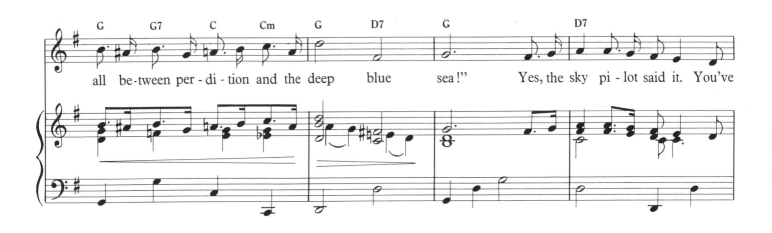

got to give him cred - it, for a son-of-a-gun of a gun - ner was

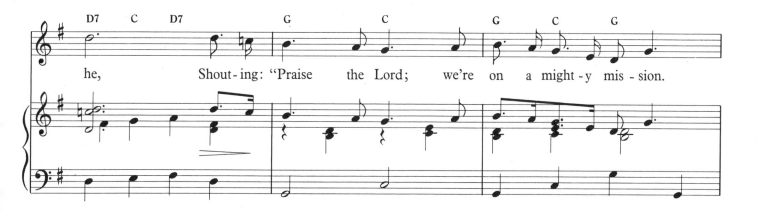

he, Shout - ing: "Praise the Lord; we're on a might - y mis - sion.

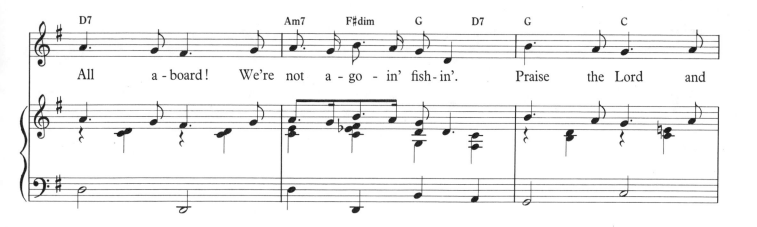

All a - board! We're not a - go - in' fish-in'. Praise the Lord and

pass the am - mu - ni - tion, and we'll all stay free!" free!"

SAN ANTONIO ROSE

Words and Music by
BOB WILLS

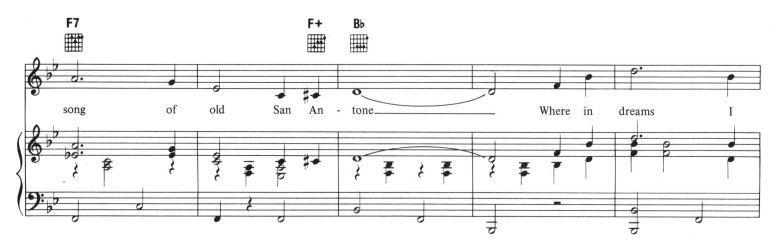

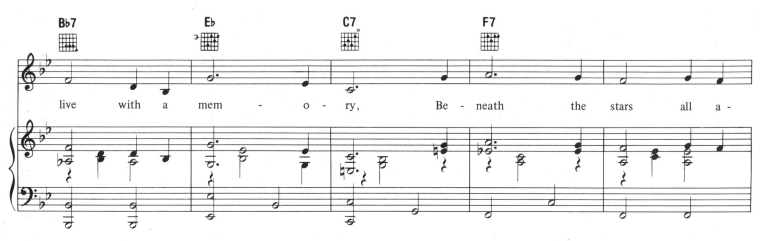

live with a mem - o - ry, Be - neath the stars all a -

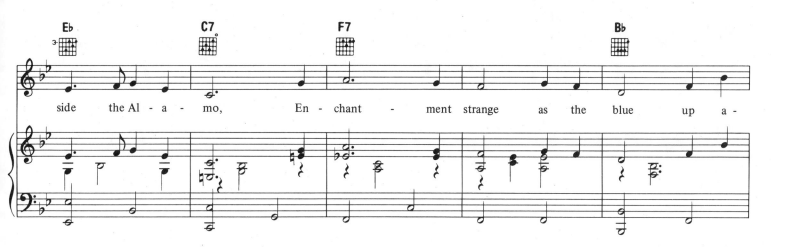

lone._____ It was there I found be -

side the Al - a - mo, En - chant - ment strange as the blue up a -

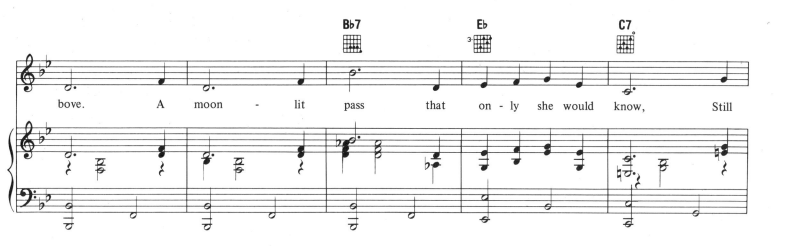

bove. A moon - lit pass that on - ly she would know, Still

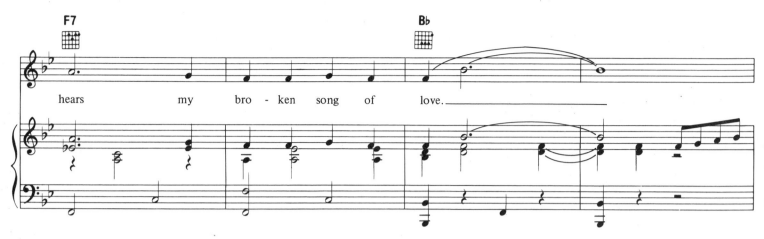

hears my bro - ken song of love.

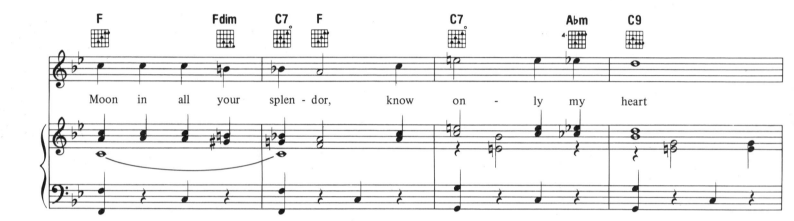

Moon in all your splen - dor, know on - ly my heart

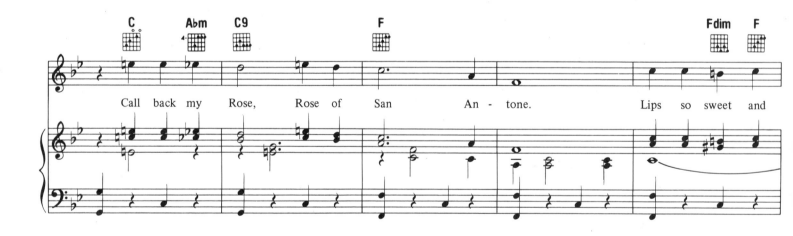

Call back my Rose, Rose of San An - tone. Lips so sweet and

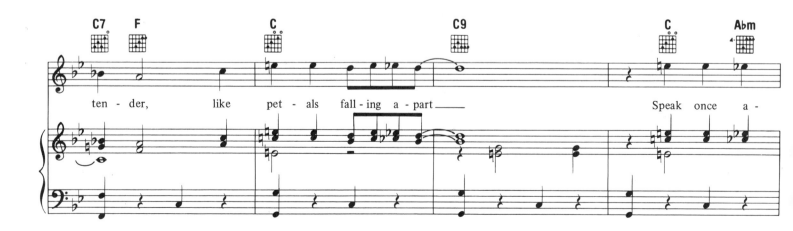

ten - der, like pet - als fall - ing a - part Speak once a -

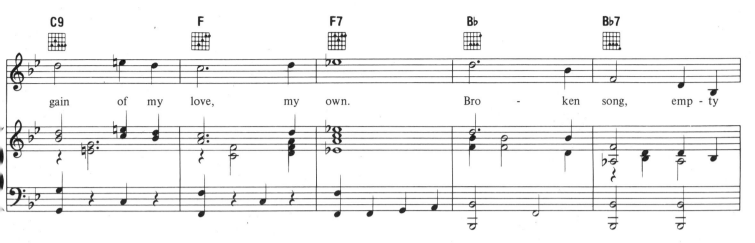

gain of my love, my own. Bro - ken song, emp - ty

words I know Still live in my heart all a - lone___

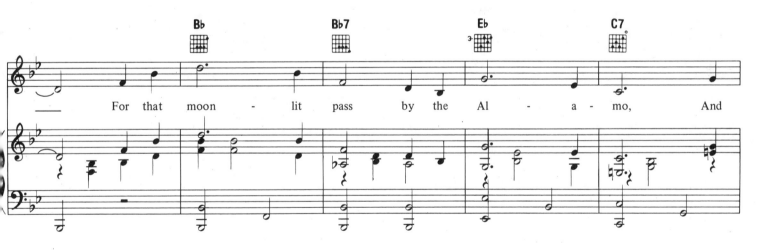

___ For that moon - lit pass by the Al - a - mo, And

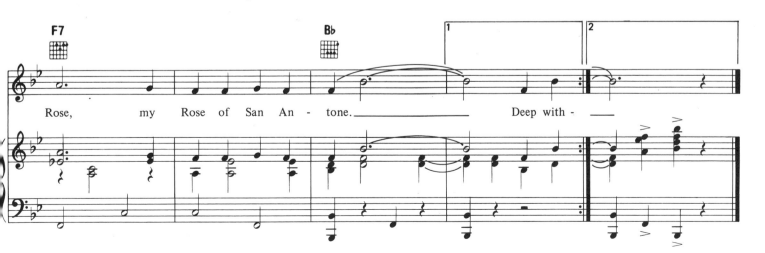

Rose, my Rose of San An - tone.___ Deep with - ___

SING ME NOT A BALLAD

(From The Musical Production "FIREBRAND OF FLORENCE")

Words by IRA GERSHWIN
Music by KURT WEILL

high life ____ Gal-lant-ry ____ I find ar - cha-ic ____

Po - et - ry ____ I find pro - sa - ic.

Give me the man who's strong and si - lent ____ In - ar - tic - u -

sempre *p*

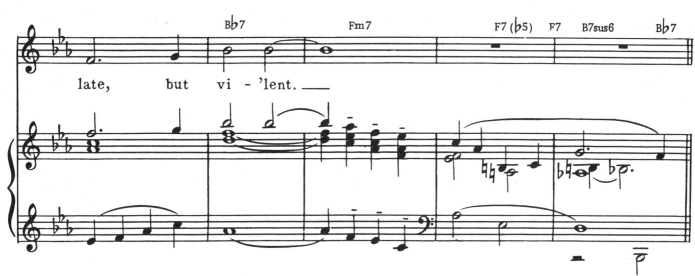

late, but vi - 'lent. ____

Refrain, Allegretto amoroso

Sing me not a bal - lad

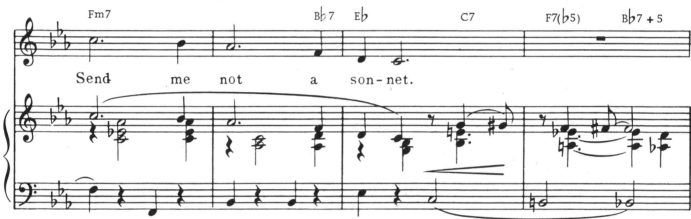

Send me not a son - net.

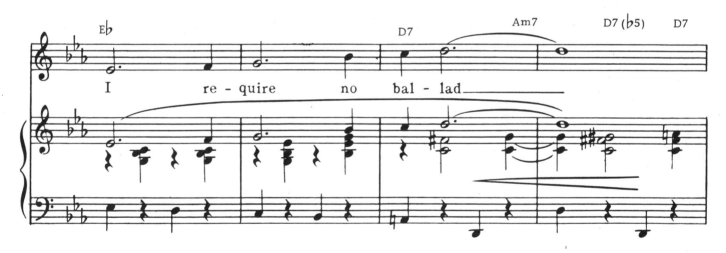

I re - quire no bal - lad

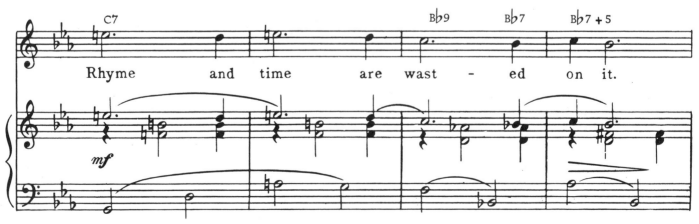

Rhyme and time are wast - ed on it.

Save your books and flow - ers ____

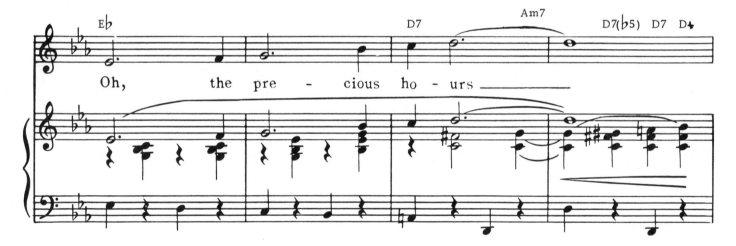

They're not ne - ces - sa - ries.

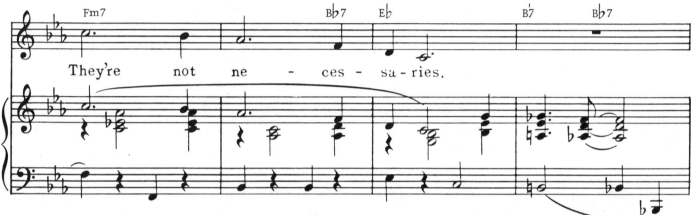

Oh, the pre - cious ho - urs ____

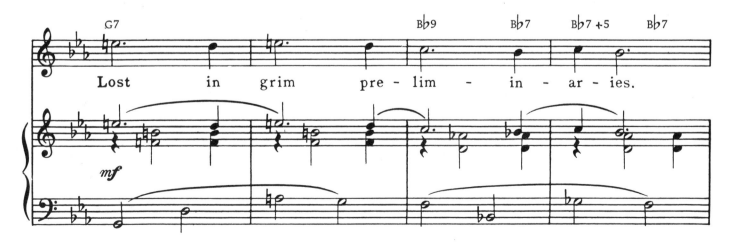

Lost in grim pre - lim - in - ar - ies.

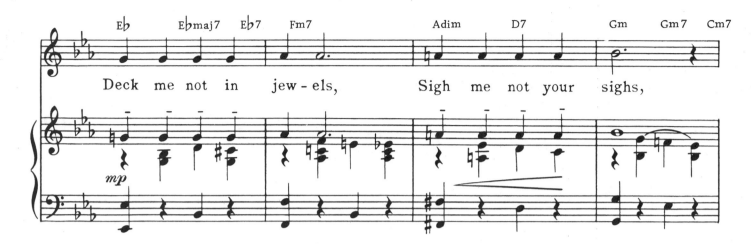

Deck me not in jew-els, Sigh me not your sighs,

Du-el me no du-els And please don't vo-cal-ize. Ro-

mance me no ro-manc-es _____ Treas-ure

not my glove_____ Spare me

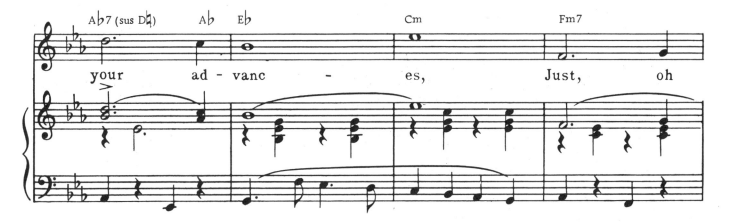

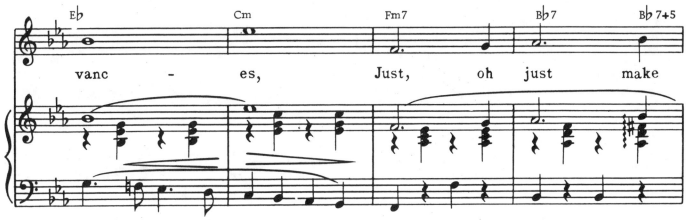

STEPPIN' OUT WITH MY BABY

(From The Motion Picture Irving Berlin's "EASTER PARADE")

Words and Music by
IRVING BERLIN

SOME ENCHANTED EVENING
(From "SOUTH PACIFIC")

Lyrics by OSCAR HAMMERSTEIN II
Music by RICHARD RODGERS

THAT OLD BLACK MAGIC

(From The Paramount Picture "STAR SPANGLED RHYTHM")

Words by JOHNNY MERCER
Music by HAROLD ARLEN

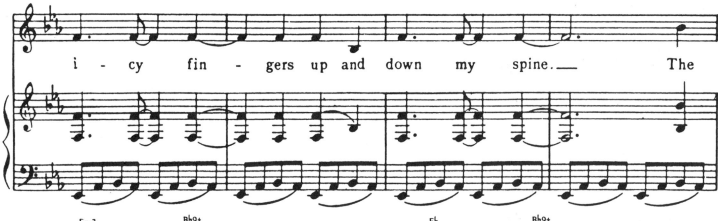

i - cy fin - gers up and down my spine.___ The

same old witch - craft when your eyes meet mine.___ The

same old tin - gle that I feel in - side___ And

then that el - e - va - tor starts its___ ride___ And

TIME AFTER TIME

(From The Metro-Goldwyn-Mayer Picture "IT HAPPENED IN BROOKLYN")

Words by SAMMY CAHN
Music by JULE STYNE

TOO DARN HOT

Words and Music by
COLE PORTER

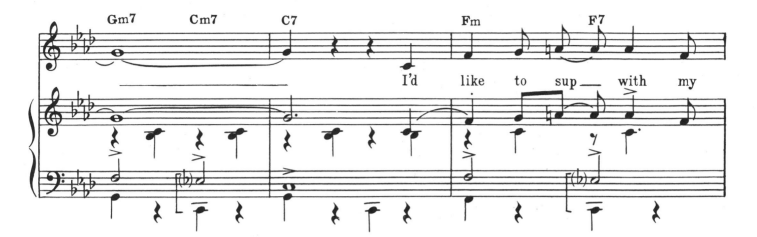

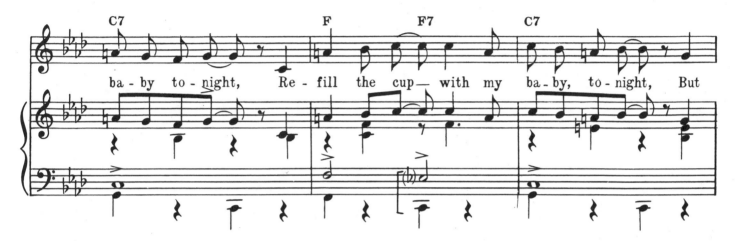

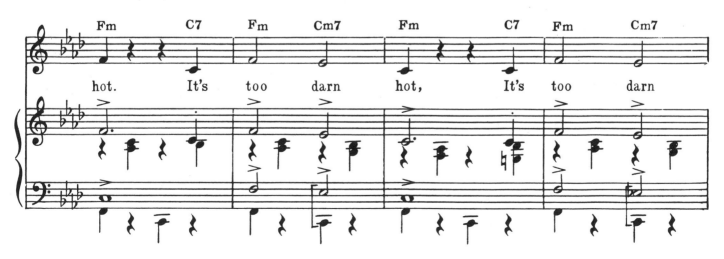

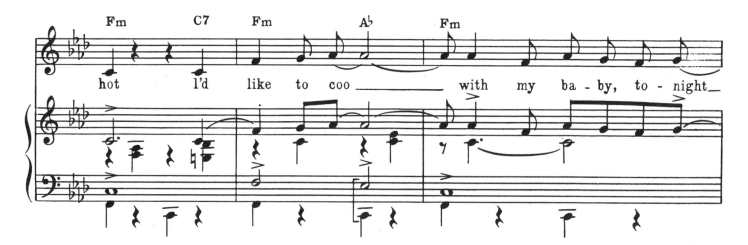

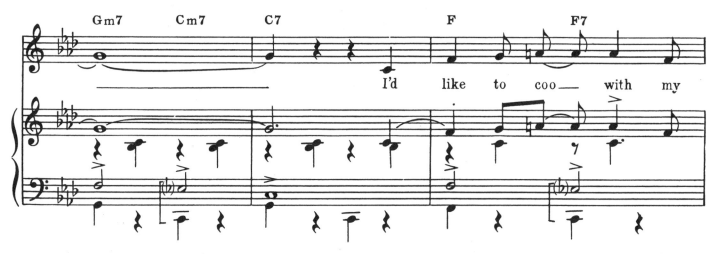

broth- er, you_fight my ba-by, to-night, 'Cause it's too darn hot.

Ac - cord-ing to the Kin - sey re-port Ev -'ry av - er-age man you

know ___ Much pre- fers his lov-ey dov - ey to court When the

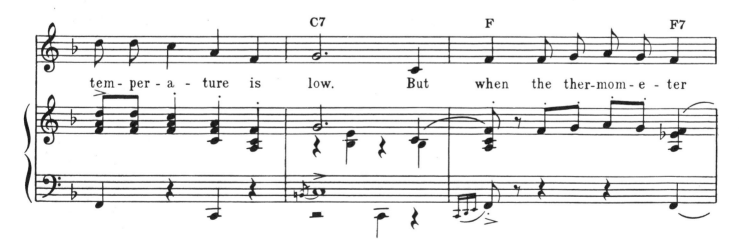

tem- per- a -ture is low. But when the ther-mom-e -ter

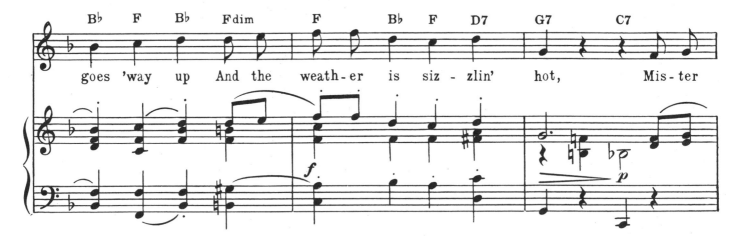

goes 'way up And the weath-er is siz-zlin' hot, Mis-ter

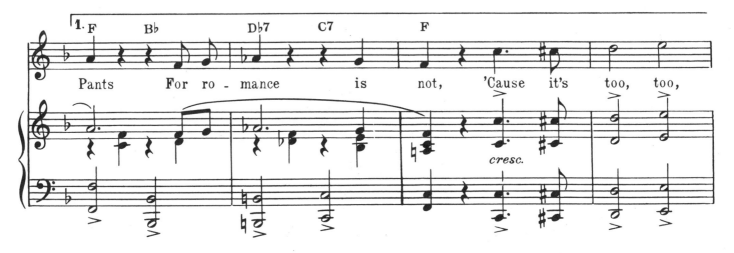

Pants For ro-mance is not, 'Cause it's too, too,

Too darn hot, It's too darn hot, It's

too darn hot. Ac-

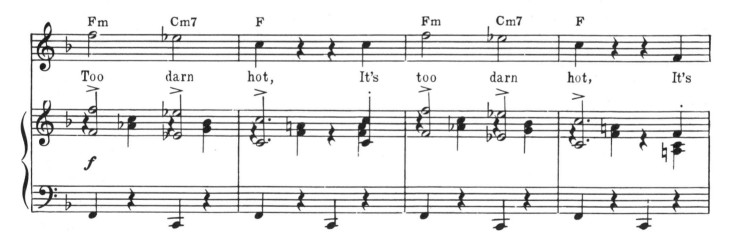

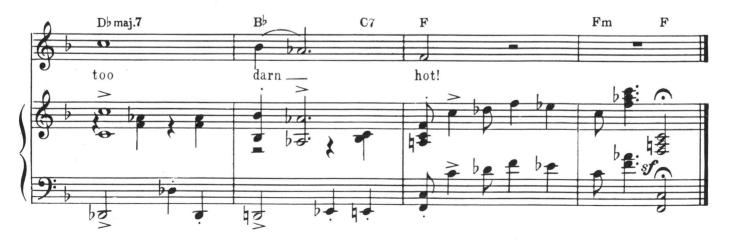

WAIT TILL YOU SEE HER

(From "BY JUPITER")

Words by LORENZ HART
Music by RICHARD RODGERS

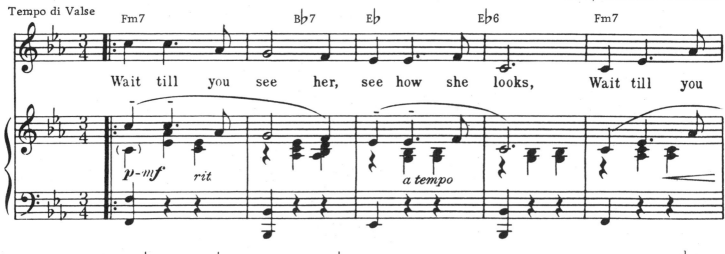

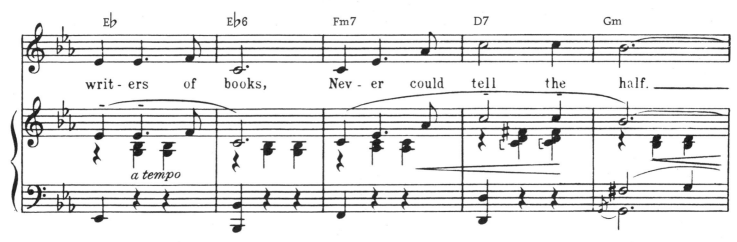

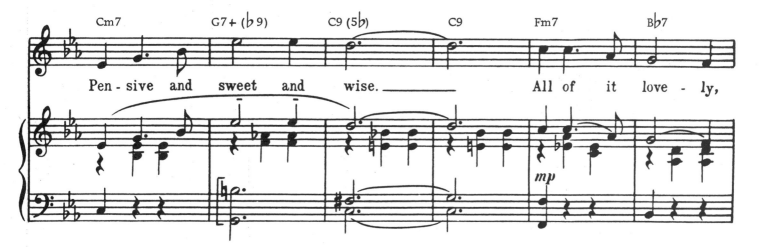

Pen - sive and sweet and wise. _____ All of it love - ly,

All of it thrill - ing; I'll nev - er be will - ing to free

her, When you see her, You won't be -

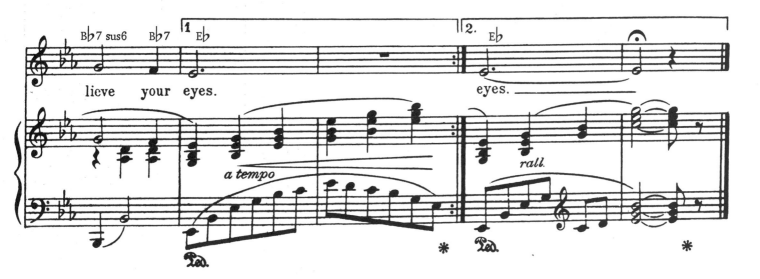

lieve your eyes. eyes. _____

YOU WERE NEVER LOVELIER

Words and Music by JOHNNY MERCER
and JEROME KERN

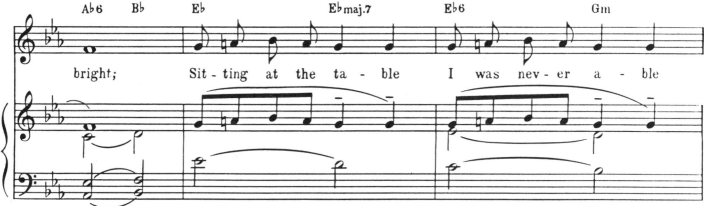

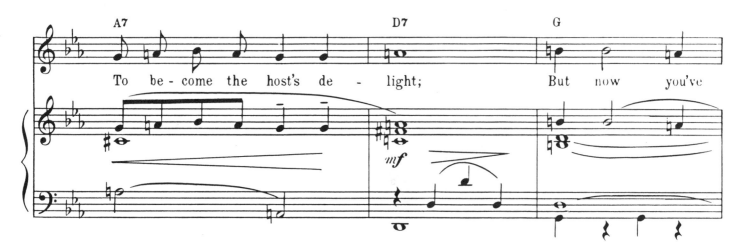

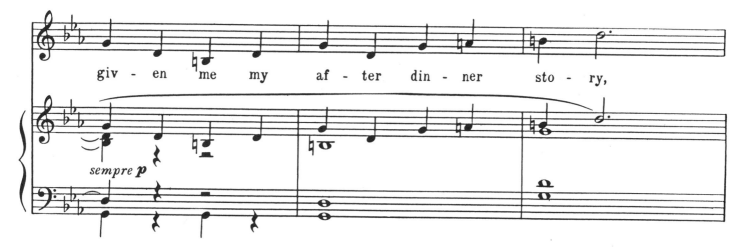

give - en me my af - ter din - ner sto - ry,

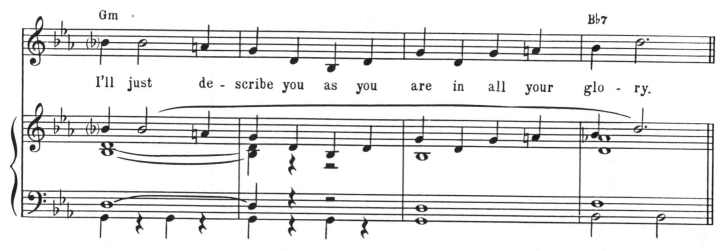

I'll just de - scribe you as you are in all your glo - ry.

Refrain (*Moderately and rhythmically*)

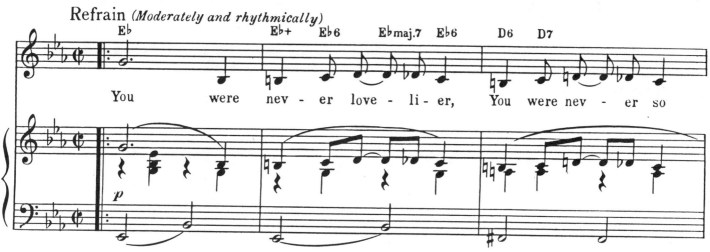

You were nev - er love - li - er, You were nev - er so

fair, Dreams were nev - er love - li - er, Par - don me_ if I

Bb9　Bb7　Eb(F)　Gb+ Ebm6　Fm7　Gm　Ab　Bb7

stare.　Down the sky the moon-beams fly to light your

Gm7　Cm7　Ab6 Abmaj.7　Bb7　Gm7　Cm　Fm7

face;　I can on-ly say they chose the pro - per

Bb9　Bb7　Eb　Eb+　Eb6　Ebmaj.7　Eb6

place.　You were nev-er love-li-er,

poco rit　*p a tempo*

Ebdim　D7　Fm7　Bb7　Eb6　Cm　Cm7

And to coin a new phrase;　I was nev-er luck-i-er

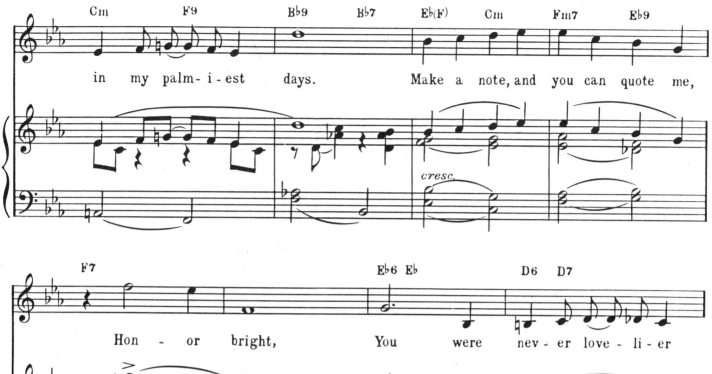

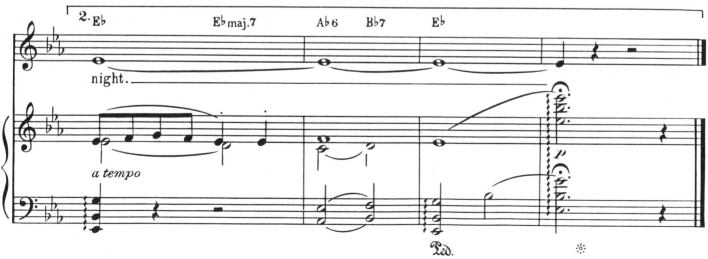

YOU'RE NEARER

(From "TOO MANY GIRLS")

Words by LORENZ HART
Music by RICHARD RODGERS

ZIP-A-DEE-DOO-DAH

(From Walt Disney's "SONG OF THE SOUTH")
(From Disneyland and Walt Disney World's "SPLASH MOUNTAIN")

Words by RAY GILBERT
Music by ALLIE WRUBEL

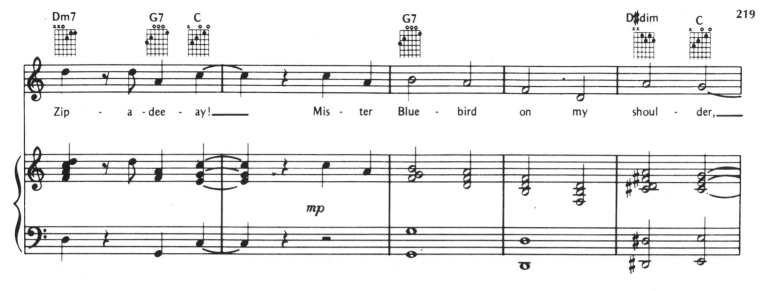

Zip - a - dee - ay!___ Mis - ter Blue - bird on my shoul - der,___

___ It's the truth, it's "act - ch'll", Ev - 'ry - thing is

TACET

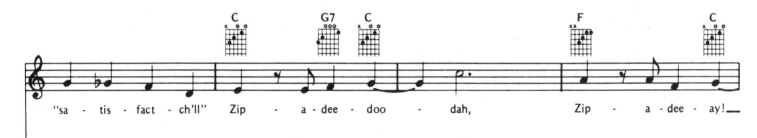

"sa - tis - fact - ch'll" Zip - a - dee - doo - dah, Zip - a - dee - ay!___

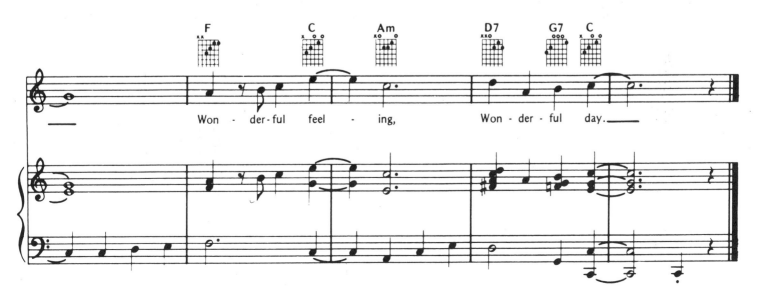

___ Won - der - ful feel - ing, Won - der - ful day.___

YOUNGER THAN SPRINGTIME
(From "SOUTH PACIFIC")

Lyrics by OSCAR HAMMERSTEIN II
Music by RICHARD RODGERS

THE DECADE SERIES

The Decade Series explores the music of the 1890s to the 1980s through each era's major events and personalities. Each volume features text and photos and over 40 of the decade's top songs, showing how music has acted as a mirror or a catalyst for current events and trends. All books are arranged for piano, voice and guitar.

Songs Of The 1890's
55 songs, including: Asleep In The Deep • Hello! Ma Baby • Maple Leaf Rag • My Wild Irish Rose • 'O Sole Mio • The Sidewalks Of New York • Stars And Stripes Forever • Ta Ra Ra Boom De Ay • When You Were Sweet Sixteen • and more.
00311655 ....$12.95

Songs Of The 1900's - 1900-1909
57 favorites, including: By The Light Of The Silvery Moon • Fascination • Give My Regards To Broadway • Glow Worm • Meet Me In St. Louis • Take Me Out To The Ball Game • Yankee Doodle Boy • and more.
00311656 ....$12.95

Songs Of The 1910's
57 classics, including: After You've Gone • Ah! Sweet Mystery Of Life • Danny Boy • Let Me Call You Sweetheart • My Melancholy Baby • Oh, You Beautiful Doll • When Irish Eyes Are Smiling • You Made Me Love You (I Didn't Want To Do It) • and more.
00311657 ....$12.95

Songs Of The 20's
58 songs, featuring: Ain't Misbehavin' • April Showers • Baby Face • California Here I Come • Five Foot Two, Eyes Of Blue • I Can't Give You Anything But Love • Manhattan • Stardust • The Varsity Drag • Who's Sorry Now.
00361122 ....$14.95

Songs Of The 30's
61 songs, featuring: All Of Me • The Continental • I Can't Get Started • I'm Getting Sentimental Over You • In The Mood • The Lady Is A Tramp • Love Letters In The Sand • My Funny Valentine • Smoke Gets In Your Eyes • What A Diff'rence A Day Made.
00361123 ....$14.95

Songs Of The 40's
61 songs, featuring: God Bless The Child • How High The Moon • The Last Time I Saw Paris • Moonlight In Vermont • A Nightingale Sang In Berkeley Square • A String Of Pearls • Swinging On A Star • Tuxedo Junction • You'll Never Walk Alone.
00361124 ....$14.95

Songs Of The 50's
59 songs, featuring: Blue Suede Shoes • Blue Velvet • Here's That Rainy Day • Love Me Tender • Misty • Rock Around The Clock • Satin Doll • Tammy • Three Coins In The Fountain • Young At Heart.
00361125 ....$14.95

Songs Of The 60's
60 songs, featuring: By The Time I Get To Phoenix • California Dreamin' • Can't Help Falling In Love • Downtown • Green Green Grass Of Home • Happy Together • I Want To Hold Your Hand • Love Is Blue • More • Strangers In The Night.
00361126 ....$14.95

Songs Of The 70's
More than 45 songs including: Don't Cry For Me Argentina • Feelings • The First Time Ever I Saw Your Face • How Deep Is Your Love • Imagine • Let It Be • Me And Bobby McGee • Piano Man • Send In The Clowns • You Don't Bring Me Flowers • You Needed Me.
00361127 ....$14.95

Songs Of The 80's
Over 40 of this decade's biggest hits, including: Candle In The Wind • Don't Worry, Be Happy • Ebony And Ivory • Endless Love • Every Breath You Take • Flashdance...What A Feeling • Islands In The Stream • Kokomo • Memory • Sailing • Somewhere Out There • We Built This City • What's Love Got To Do With It • With Or Without You.
00490275 ....$14.95

MORE SONGS OF THE DECADE SERIES

Due to popular demand, we are pleased to present these new collections with even more great songs from the 1920s through 1980s. Each book features beautiful piano/vocal/guitar arrangements. Perfect for practicing musicians, educators, collectors, and music hobbyists.

More Songs Of The 20's
Over 50 songs, including: Ain't We Got Fun? • Bill • Carolina In The Morning • Fascinating Rhythm • The Hawaiian Wedding Song • Malaguena • Nobody Knows You When You're Down And Out • Someone To Watch Over Me • Yes, Sir, That's My Baby • and more.
00311647 ....$14.95

More Songs of the 30's
Over 50 songs, including: All The Things You Are • A Fine Romance • In A Sentimental Mood • Just A Gigolo • Let's Call The Whole Thing Off • Mad Dogs And Englishmen • Stompin' At The Savoy • Stormy Weather • Thanks For The Memory • and more.
00311648 ....$14.95

More Songs Of The 40's
Over 60 songs, including: Bali Ha'i • Be Careful, It's My Heart • Five Guys Named Moe • The Last Time I Saw Paris • Old Devil Moon • San Antonio Rose • Some Enchanted Evening • Too Darn Hot • and more.
00311649 ....$14.95

More Songs Of The 50's
56 songs, including: Blueberry Hill • Chanson D'Amour • Charlie Brown • Do-Re-Mi • Hey, Good Lookin' • Hound Dog • I Could Have Danced All Night • Mack The Knife • Mona Lisa • My Favorite Things • (Let Me Be Your) Teddy Bear • That's Amore • and more.
00311650 ....$14.95

FOR MORE INFORMATION, SEE YOUR LOCAL MUSIC DEALER,
OR WRITE TO:

HAL•LEONARD™
CORPORATION
7777 W. BLUEMOUND RD. P.O. BOX 13819 MILWAUKEE, WI 53213

Prices, contents, and availability subject to change without notice
Some products may not be available outside the U.S.A.

More Songs Of The 60's
66 songs, including: Alfie • Baby Elephant Walk • Bonanza • Born To Be Wild • Eleanor Rigby • Moon River • Raindrops Keep Fallin' On My Head • Seasons In The Sun • Sweet Caroline • Tell Laura I Love Her • What The World Needs Now • Wooly Bully • and more.
00311651 ....$14.95

More Songs Of The 70's
Over 50 songs, including: Afternoon Delight • All By Myself • American Pie • Billy, Don't Be A Hero • Happy Days • Honesty • I Shot The Sheriff • Maggie May • Maybe I'm Amazed • She Believes In Me • She's Always A Woman • Wishing You Were Here • and more.
00311652 ....$14.95

More Songs Of The 80's
43 songs, including: Addicted To Love • Call Me • Don't Know Much • Footloose • Girls Just Want To Have Fun • The Heat Is On • Karma Chameleon • Longer • Straight Up • Take My Breath Away • Tell Her About It • We're In This Love Together • and more.
00311653 ....$14.95

STILL MORE SONGS OF THE DECADE SERIES

What could be better than even *more* songs from your favorite decade! These books feature piano/vocal/guitar arrangements with no duplication with *earlier volumes*.

Still More Songs Of The 30's
Over 50 songs including: April in Paris • Body And Soul • Heat Wave • It Don't Mean A Thing (If It Ain't Got That Swing) • and more.
00310027 ....$14.95

Still More Songs Of The 40's
Over 50 songs including: Any Place I Hang My Hat • Don't Get Around Much Anymore • If I Loved You • Sentimental Journey • and more.
00310028 ....$14.95

Still More Songs Of The 50's
Over 50 songs including: Autumn Leaves • Chantilly Lace • If I Were A Bell • Luck Be A Lady • The Man That Got Away • Venus • and more.
00310029 ....$14.95

Still More Songs Of The 60's
Over 50 more songs, including: Do You Know The Way To San Jose • Duke Of Earl • Hey Jude • I'm Henry VIII, I Am • Leader Of The Pack • (You Make Me Feel) Like A Natural Woman • What A Wonderful World • and more.
00311680 ....$14.95

Still More Songs Of The 70's
Over 60 hits, including: Cat's In The Cradle • Nadia's Theme • Philadelphia Freedom • The Way We Were • You've Got A Friend • and more.
00311683 ....$14.95